Raspberry Pi
Master Series

Raspberry Pi 4 Ultimate Guide
From Beginner to Pro

&

Raspberry Pi 4 Project Workbook

Ethan J. Upton

Raspberry Pi 4 Ultimate Guide From Beginner to Pro:

Everything You Need to Know: Setup, Programming Theory, Techniques, and Awesome Ideas to Build Your Own Projects

Ethan J. Upton

Table of Contents

Introduction

Congratulations on purchasing Raspberry Pi 4 Ultimate Guide, and thank you for doing so.

There are plenty of books on this subject on the market, thanks again for choosing this one! Every effort was made to ensure it is full of as much useful information as possible, please enjoy!

A book does not aspire to give deep theoretical knowledge but has a strictly practical orientation. We will show you what the Raspberry Pi includes, how to configure it, and how to use it to make your own projects. The examples are intended to be approachable even by first-year students who have already completed the Computer Science course.

An important incorporation in this edition of the book is the notions of software architecture. We want Raspberry Pi to be used to address real engineering problems. And for that, it is necessary that the software developed be considerably more evolved than what we usually see in the final degree projects. The examples we will address are simple but not trivial. Reusable component templates will be provided to build relatively sophisticated systems.

Info: All the code we give you with the book can be used in your own works and projects. It is distributed under the GNU public license, a permissive license that allows you to even modify the software or commercially exploit your projects. There is only one condition, and derivative works can only be distributed under this license.

An important limitation of this book is that we do not deal with strict real-time systems, but we cannot do more in two credits. In the near future, we will try to offer complementary real-time and robotics courses with Raspberry Pi.

Student Kit

This book is conceived as a pro-bono motivation activity, without any remuneration for the personnel involved in the course. 100% of the money raised in the tuition is invested in the material that the student takes. Purchases are made months in advance, thanks to the collaboration of the School of Industrial Engineering of Toledo, to take advantage of offers and foreign suppliers.

Book Structure

This book is divided into three parts:
The first part introduces the Raspberry Pi, its characteristics, its history, the operating system that we are going to use, and the development environment.
The second part describes the different components of the Raspberry Pi from an isolated point of view. It is about the student knowing how each component is programmed and what limitations it has. Finally, the last part is dedicated to software architecture issues. How we build programs that deal with multiple sources of heterogeneous events. How a complex program is organized so that it is not impossible to modify it.

Organization of this book

This little book has been divided into three parts:

- The first part is dedicated to the fundamentals and necessary introduction material. Ideally, the student should have at least this knowledge at the beginning of the book, but we will dedicate the first day to review them.

- The second part introduces peripherals and peripheral programming from an agnostic point of view regarding language. Command-line tools are used to interact with them.

- The third part is dedicated to the programming of the Raspberry Pi. Two versions are offered, one in C and one in Python. It includes material of foundations, simple examples equivalent to the second part, and case studies.

Obviously, this organization is influenced by practical aspects. We leave for the second part all the common material that we can, so as not to repeat it in the third parts C and Python. In the book, we see everything together, presenting parallel versions C and Python.

Chapter 1 - Raspberry Pi

In 2006, a group from the Computer Lab of the University of Cambridge began to worry about the level with which high school students arrived at the University. For some reason, students who had previous exposure to computer technologies accumulated knowledge about specific applications rather than knowledge about the technologies themselves. Raspberry Pi emerges as a low-cost initiative to promote experimentation with programming from an early age, although this is not a mere toy.

The Raspberry Pi Family

In the timeline above, you can see a set of the most significant milestones related to Raspberry Pi. A respectable number of models have already been generated in the short history of the Raspberry Pi Foundation:

- Raspberry Pi model B was the first model put up for sale on February 29, 2012. The original design included two models with the same printed circuit. Both were designed around a Broadcom SoC (System On a Chip), the BCM2835 at 700MHz, designed for mobile applications that require video processing or 3D graphics (video cameras, media players, mobile phones, etc.). Most of the input/output pins of the BCM2835 were arranged in a 26-pin header. Model B was the high-end, developer-oriented version with more memory (512MB of RAM versus 256MB), a 100BaseTX Ethernet port, and a USB hub with two USB 2.0 ports. The original models incorporated an SD slot. In September 2012, the design was slightly revised to correct some problems. This revision slightly modifies the available input/output pins.

- Raspberry Pi model A is the reduced version of the model B. It incorporates half of RAM than the B model (256MB), does not include an Ethernet interface and only incorporates a USB 2.0 port. It is intended for final applications where consumption and/or cost are important factors.

- The Raspberry Pi logo is a registered trademark of the Raspberry Pi Foundation. It was designed by Paul Bleech, who won the logo competition organized by the foundation in 2011. Most of the candidates are still available in the forum of the foundation. Beware of the logo; it has very strict rules of use. You cannot use it where you see fit.

- In April 2014, the Raspberry Pi Compute Module is announced. It is similar to the B model, but instead of the SD slot, it incorporates 4GB of eMMC Flash and integrates everything into a DDR2 SODIMM printed circuit, similar to that of notebook memories. This allows all the pins of the BCM2835 to be available but requires another printed circuit with the SODIMM socket and the necessary connectors. It is used extensively in the development of products based on Raspberry Pi, such as the FiveNinjas Slice media player, the CubeSat satellites, the Otto camera, the Cube Solver that is capable of solving a Rubik, Sphinx cube that is used to use a tablet as a desktop computer, etc.

- In July 2014, the Raspberry Pi model B + is announced. It is a redesign of model B, very similar but with important consequences. The number of GPIO header pins is expanded to 40 pins, the SD socket is replaced by a microSD, the number of USB ports is increased to four, the power and audio are improved, the output is included in the same connector of composite video and audio (like many laptops), and the form factor is corrected so that it fits completely into the size of a credit card. The extension of the pin header is complemented shortly afterwards with the specification HAT (Hardware Attached on Top). Compute Module IO Board with the module inserted, which determines the physical and electrical limitations that Raspberry Pi expansion boards must meet to ensure future compatibility. All Raspberry Pi will be compatible with this specification from this date. HAT allows automatic configuration of digital inputs/outputs as well as drivers through two dedicated pins (ID_SD and ID_SC). Today, there are many HATs on the market (as an example, see the collection of Adafruit, Pimoroni, and The Pi Hut). In addition to the BCM2835, the B + model incorporates an SMS95 LAN9514 that incorporates the Ethernet interface and the USB hub occupying a single USB port of the BCM2835.

- In November 2014, the Raspberry Pi A + as the equivalent redesign of model A, without SMSC LAN9514. A significant change is that the idea of using the same printed circuit is abandoned. In this way, it is possible to reduce the size significantly and with it the price. It incorporates the HAT header, which will already be present in all subsequent models, and consumption is significantly reduced.

- Almost on the third anniversary of the original Raspberry Pi, the Raspberry Pi 4 is announced. Upgrade the processor to a BCM2836 (quad-core Cortex-A7) at 900MHz and incorporate 1GB of RAM. For the first time, the possibility of using Microsoft Windows 10 on Raspberry Pi opens, although the operating system recommended by the Raspberry Pi Foundation remains Raspbian.

- This is a tiny version of the A + model with greater speed (1GHz) and more memory (512MB). Without populating the baseboards, the price was lowered to $ 5. The 40th issue of The MagPi magazine included a Raspberry Pi 4 gift. It seems that Google's pressure after a meeting of Eric Schmidt and Eben Upton was decisive in its development. However, it is a model produced directly by Raspberry Pi Trading, which has relatively limited production capacity, making it difficult to achieve.

- In 2019, the Raspberry Pi 4 B is announced, coinciding with the fourth birthday of the Raspberry Pi original model B. The change is very important because it is passed to a 64-bit architecture, although backward compatibility remains total. In addition to the BCM2837, it incorporates a BCM43438 that implements all the new wireless communication capabilities. Just leave the FM radio receiver unconnected.

- In February 2016, Eben Upton announced in various forums that a Compute Module 3 is being prepared, and it will be a Raspberry Pi 4. The specifications are not public yet, but beta versions are already available for some engineers.

If you want to know more about the history of Raspberry Pi and its community, we recommend you visit the website of The MagPi magazine. It is a magazine of great quality and completely free in its electronic version. It is also a very interesting source of suppliers of products related to Raspberry Pi.

Broadcom Chip Systems

This on-chip system incorporates a low-power ARM1176JZF-S core and a VideoCore IV dual-core multimedia coprocessor

(GPU). The GPU implements OpenGL-ES 2.0 and is capable of encoding and decoding FullHD video at 30fps while displaying FullHD graphics at 60fps on an LCD or on an HDMI monitor. A striking feature of this processor is its assembly stacked with RAM (package on package). The structure is shown in the figure. For this reason, the Raspberry Pi printed circuit does not show any processor. This technique allows for reducing the size of the PCB considerably.

This on-chip system incorporates a low-power ARM1176JZF-S core and a VideoCore IV dual-core multimedia coprocessor (GPU). The GPU implements OpenGL-ES 2.0 and is capable of encoding and decoding FullHD video at 30fps while displaying FullHD graphics at 60fps on an LCD or on an HDMI monitor. A striking feature of this processor is its assembly stacked with RAM (package on package). For this reason, the Raspberry Pi printed circuit does not show any processor.

This technique allows for reducing considerably the size of the PCB (Printed Circuit Board) necessary. In addition to the processor and the GPU, the Raspberry Pi SoC incorporates a wide array of peripherals:

- Timer
- Interrupt controller
- Generic purpose digital inputs/outputs, GPIO (General Purpose Input-Output). It has 54, but not all are available on the Raspberry Pi.
- USB port.
- PCM audio via the I2S bus (Integrated Interchip Sound).
- Direct memory access controller, DMA.
- Master and slave of I2C bus (Inter-Integrated Circuit).
- SPI bus master and slave (Serial Peripheral Interface).
- Module for generating variable width pulses, PWM.
- Serial ports, UART.

- Interface for eMMC, SD, SDIO memories.
- HDMI interface

Applying reverse engineering techniques, a substantial part of the GPU was documented in the Herman Hermitage GitHub repository. This work may have influenced Broadcom's recent decision to release the official VideoCore IV documentation. Advanced users can now enjoy reasonably mature development libraries and an accelerated OpenGL driver completely free.

The BCM2836 of the Raspberry Pi 4 has basically the same internal architecture as its predecessor but incorporates a quad-core Cortex-A7 processor that replaces the ARM117JZF-S of the BCM2835 and does not use the package-on-package assembly technique. It has important consequences from the point of view of the software since this processor implements the instruction repertoire of ARM v.7 instead of ARM v.6 as its predecessor.

The BCM2837 of the Raspberry Pi 4 B is an on-chip system designed specifically for this Raspberry Pi model. It updates the processor for four 64-bit Cortex-A53 cores but continues to incorporate the VideoCore IV GPU because it is one of the few GPUs with public documentation from the manufacturer.

The ARM Cortex-A53 has an internal name Apollo and is often used in high-performance processors in combination with the ARM Cortex-A57 (Atlas) following the big.LITTLE (heterogeneous multiprocessor) configuration. The A53 is the version of low consumption, reduced size, and relative simplicity of the ARMv8 architecture, while A57 is the version of high performance, high consumption, and larger size of the same architecture. For example, the Exynos 7 Octa or Snapdragon 810 that incorporate many high-end mobile phones follow this configuration using four cores of each type. In the case of BCM2837, it is decided to include only four low-consumption cores, so it does not intend to compete in high performance, but in energy efficiency. Basically, the expected performance is somewhat better than a quad-core Cortex-A9 (for example, like the Apple iPad 2 processor) but at a significantly lower cost.

A Raspberry Pi for the Book

This initiation book could be carried out on any Raspberry Pi model. The new Raspberry Pi 4 is ideal for equipment prototypes, but it makes development difficult. For example, connecting a keyboard and mouse would require a USB OTG hub. The mere update of the operating system would require some kind of network connection, and connecting external devices to the GPIO port requires incorporating pin headers or soldering. All this is already in the Raspberry Pi model B +.

The added cost of all the additional components that would be necessary to incorporate the Raspberry Pi 4 to develop comfortably far exceeds the cost of the Raspberry Pi B +.

Unfortunately, the price of the B + model is rising due to the fall in demand since the Raspberry Pi 4 is launched. At this juncture, the Raspberry Pi 4 B is released at the same price as the Raspberry Pi 4, but also including WiFi and Bluetooth interface. For this reason, we decided to include the new Raspberry 3 model B in this edition. However, all book examples are compatible with any of the models.

Interoperability with Other Products

Around the Raspberry Pi Foundation has emerged a huge community of users of all levels that generates information and products. Today there are specific peripherals of all kinds for Raspberry Pi. There are cameras, touch panels with TFT screen, and many interface cards with other devices.

It is worth noting the efforts to integrate peripherals from other platforms that already enjoyed a wide user community. For example, Lego Mindstorms peripherals and LEGO Technic parts can be used to build Raspberry Pi controlled robots using BrickPi from Dexter Industries.

The huge variety of Arduino expansion modules (shields) can also be used with GertDuino from Gert van Loo, or with Arduberry from Dexter Industries, or with AlaMode from WyoLum or with ArduPi from Cooking Hacks. The tandem of Raspberry Pi and Arduino is very interesting when strict latency control is required. The Raspbian GNU / Linux operating system is not real-time, it cannot guarantee very low interrupt latencies, and the resolution of the timers is of the order of milliseconds. However, the greater simplicity of Arduino software makes it very predictable in terms of response times.

Finally, we would like to mention the Raspberry Pi to Grove interfaces, modular and open architecture for building LEGO-style electronic systems in physical systems. Grove was initially designed to be compatible with Arduino, and therefore can be used together with the adapters mentioned above, but can also be used directly using GrovePi from Dexter Industries, a shield base specially designed for Raspberry Pi.

Chapter 2 - The GNU / Linux System

The Raspberry Pi has a complete operating system, with graphics environment and programming tools of various types. We will use this environment to carry out most of the book. However, we must specify that the usual way of developing embedded systems is to use a PC and program the Raspberry Pi remotely.

GNU / Linux is the usual name of the operating system that the Raspberry Pi carries. Raspbian and Debian are nothing more than distributions of this operating system. That is, Raspbian is a selection of GNU / Linux packages, compiled for a specific architecture, and packaged with the help of specific tools to achieve a pleasant user experience. Instead of going here and there in search of installers and drivers as we do in Microsoft Windows, GNU specializes in packages for specific purposes.

GNU is the correct name of the operating system. It means GNU's Not Unix, that is, GNU is not Unix. It is a recursive acronym. It refers to the fact that it does not contain a single line of Unix, the proprietary operating system of AT&T, which then sold to SCO and licensed to multiple international brands. The Linux suffix refers to the kernel of the operating system. GNU has its own kernel, the HURD, but is not yet ready for general use. That's why most distributions add to GNU some of the free kernels out there (Linux, FreeBSD, NetBSD, etc.)

Info: In 1983, Richard M. Stallman, who worked as a researcher at the AI Lab at MIT, decided to start the GNU project in order to make unnecessary the use of any other non-free software. It is still far from reaching its goal, but GNU is already used in many electronic devices. You can read more about the initial objective of the project, The GNU Manifesto.

In 1985 he created the Free Software Foundation with the aim of spreading the free software movement and helping the development of the GNU system. Listen to Richard Stallman himself explaining the philosophy of the movement.

As soon as you connect the Raspberry Pi to the power, it will start in a graphic environment like the one at the beginning of the chapter. The following elements appear at the top.

- Applications menu
- Order line terminal.
- Raspberry Pi configuration tool.
- File management tool.
- Integrated Python development environment (IDLE).
- Text editor
- Basic web browser.

From the menu, it is possible to run most of the installed applications. However, with the quick launch buttons of applications, we will have enough for most of the book activities.

The File System

Let's first get acquainted with the structure of folders and files of the system. To do this, click on the quick launch button of the file manager.

The text box at the top indicates /home /pi, which is the current folder. The routes of the files and folders use the character / as a separator. It's not possible to have a folder with that character in the name because the system could not differentiate it from a route of two components. The folder / without more is the root folder, where everything hangs. Not here. Here, there are unit names, all units are seen at some point in the tree of folders that are born in the root folder. The route /home/pi refers to being found in the pi folder of the File Manager. As you can imagine, it is the personal folder. The name 'home' refers to the folder containing all the personal folders (home in English). And inside that folder, the folder pi is that of the user pi. Indeed, pi is the name of the user created folder by default in the system when installed. In the book, we will use this user exclusively, but we encourage you to become your own user. You will see that in this folder, there are already some files. They are examples of programs in several programming languages, which we will use in the course.

Although the system does not require it, the different variants of GNU tend to maintain a common folder structure.

For example, the following are usually present in almost all GNU systems:

/ home / Personal folders of users.
/ root / Personal folder of the administrator (root user).
/ etc / System configuration files.
/ boot / Files needed for system boot.
/ bin / Basic orders (system executables).
/ usr / bin / Rest of system orders (executables).
/ lib / Basic system libraries
/ usr / lib / Other system libraries.
/ usr / local / Software installed manually, not belonging to the system.
/ tmp / Temporary folder.
/ dev / System devices. In GNU all devices are viewed as special files.

Use the file manager to navigate the system and familiarize yourself with it. Do not worry, as a pi user, you cannot destroy anything essential to the system. We propose the following exercises:

1. Find the file wpa_supplicant.conf. This is the file where you can configure the WiFi network so that the Raspberry Pi automatically connects to your access point.
2. Find the flickering.py file that is an example program written in Python that we will use in the course.
3. Find the gcc program. This is the C compiler.
4. Find the idle program. This is the integrated programming environment with Python.

Warning

Traditionally in operating systems, the term directory is used to refer to a folder. In the same way, many texts in Spanish speak of files to refer to files. We will try to use the term folder that best fits the metaphor of the desktop.

A file is one of those cardboard folders that get into office filing cabinets. The problem is that the files cannot also be called a folder. That is why more neutral translations were sought. The file is really the archive, rather than the contents of the archive. But we warn you because in the documentation you read there, it is easy for them to appear. The directory is the same as a folder, and the file is the same as file.

The Command-Line Environment

Execute the command line terminal by clicking on the corresponding icon. Although apparently, it is a primitive interface, this is one of the most flexible ways to communicate with the operating system.

Pressing the icon, we will see that a new window opens. That window corresponds to the terminal simulator program. It behaves like an old console with a keyboard and alphanumeric screen. In turn, the terminal program runs another program that is responsible for interpreting textual commands, the shell.

In GNU / Linux, the shell that is normally used is called bash (Bourne Again Shell). It has many features that make it a complete programming language by itself. We will not see the advanced features, but some basic notions that will allow you to unfold with ease during the course.

When the shell is executed, a small text appears before the cursor; it is the prompt.

Raspberry Pi pi @: ~ $ ▄

Before the colon appears, the user and the name of the computer simulating an email address. Before the @ symbol, the name of the user who runs the shell appears. In this case, the user is pi, which is the default user, and the one we will use in our examples. Then the hostname appears, which we have configured in the installation as rpi.

After the colon and before the $ symbol,   the work folder appears. The working folder (or directory) is that folder in which the shell is currently located. All processes have a working folder, and the shell is no exception. It is used as a basis to determine the files that are located by relative paths. We will see this right away.

The ~ symbol is an abbreviation for the user's home folder. In this case / home / pi. This abbreviation can be used in any order that needs a route.

There are many highly recommended references to understand the shell and exploit its full potential. An excellent book available for free is available at tldp.org.

File Management

All operations that can be performed with the file manager can also be performed with commands in the shell. Let's see a brief summary of the most frequent orders.

File list: ls

The most basic file management operation is to display the contents of a folder. It is done with the ls (list) command.

Without further arguments, it shows the contents of the working folder (the one that appears in the prompt).

The colors of each element tell us what it is. Folders are shown in blue, normal files in gray, and executables in green. By default, it does not show hidden elements, which are those whose name begins with. (point). You can indicate as an argument the folder or folders whose content you want to list:

pi @ raspberrypi: ~ $ ls src
c python README.md
Raspberry Pi pi @: ~ $ ▄

It is assumed that you want to list the src folder within the current folder. It is what is known as a relative path and is assumed to be relative to the working folder. You can also indicate the full path /home/pi/src, which is known as the absolute path. As we said before, the symbol ~ is an abbreviation of the user's home folder. Therefore, another way to express the full path would be ~ / src.

And to see hidden files and folders you can use the -a option:

pi @ raspberrypi: ~ $ ls src -a
... c.git python README.md

Raspberry Pi pi @: ~ $ ▄

In this case, the .git folder is hidden. Dot folders have a special meaning for the operating system and appear in all system folders. Folder. it represents the same folder in which it is located, and the folder.. represents the folder that contains the one shown. In our example, the src /.. folder is /home/pi while the.. folder would be / home. The src/folder. It is the same as./src, the same as src and the same as /home/pi/ src in our example.

Like all other orders, ls allows you to specify various options that modify their behavior. These options are preceded by a hyphen and can be combined or indicated separately.

If this option has not resolved your doubts, use man (book). It is a tool available in all Unix variants to consult the electronic version of the reference book. And if you have doubts about how to use man? Don't think about it, use man - help, and if it's not enough, remember that to exit man, you have to press the q (quit) key.

We have installed the book pages in Spanish. If there is help in Spanish, you will see it in Spanish. If not, practice English, if you use Raspberry Pi, it will be very useful to know English.

In some cases, there are several book pages for the same concept. For example, printf is a shell order, but it is also a C function, and you probably have the version in Spanish and English. The book pages are grouped into sections, the original sections of the Unix reference book. You can tell man what section you want to refer (a number from 1 to 9) to. For example:

pi @ raspberrypi: ~ $ man 3 printf
You have the complete list of sections on the man book page, and you don't need to know it by heart.

Some man options worth highlighting:

Option	Meaning
-k	Search for the keyword indicated in the book pages and show the ones that contain it
-K	Show all applicable book pages
-to	Pipes and redirects

The standard output of a program may be too large. So big that even with the terminal scroll bar, you could see everything. In those cases, you may be interested in redirecting the output to a file for reading carefully with an editor. For example, we will generate a file with all the executables of the system:

```
pi @ raspberrypi: ~ $ ls -1 / bin> exe-bin.txt
pi @ raspberrypi: ~ $ ls -1 / usr / bin> exe-usr-bin.txt
pi @ raspberrypi: ~ $ ls -1 / usr / local / bin> exe-usr-local-
bin.txt
Raspberry Pi pi @: ~ $ ▄
```

When using the symbol >, we are telling the shell that when I have to write something by standard output, write it in the indicated file. In our example, when the ls program executes a call to printf or similar, what it writes goes directly at the end of the indicated file. Now we can see these files carefully using an editor, such as Leafpad:

```
pi @ raspberrypi: ~ $ leafpad exe-bin.txt
```

And if we want to count how many executables the system has in total? We could use the wc program that counts, among other things, the lines of a file.

For example:
```
pi @ raspberrypi: ~ $ wc -l exe - *. txt
```

158 exe-bin.txt
1168 exe-usr-bin.txt
1 exe-usr-local-bin.txt
1327 total
Raspberry Pi pi @: ~ $ ▪

We can also redirect the standard input of a program. For example:
pi @ raspberrypi: ~ $ wc -l <exe-bin.txt
158
pi @ raspberrypi: ~ $ wc -l <exe-usr-bin.txt
1168
pi @ raspberrypi: ~ $ wc -l <exe-usr-local-bin.txt
Raspberry Pi pi @: ~ $ ▪

Now wc does not indicate any file name because it does not know it; the content of the file arrives directly when calling scanf or something similar. The good thing is that the result is a simple number that may be more convenient for other things.

But if we are interested in knowing how many executables there are and we are not interested in what specific files they are, why do we keep the list of executables in files? GNU is possible to connect the standard output of a program to the standard input of another program establishing what is known as a pipe (pipe in English):
pi @ raspberrypi: ~ $ ls -1 / bin / usr / bin / usr / local / bin | wc -l 1327
Raspberry Pi pi @: ~ $ ▪

The symbol | connects the standard output of the order on the left with the standard input of the order on the right. Even if we want to examine the list of executables, we can use this construction to avoid having to save the intermediate file:

pi @ raspberrypi: ~ $ ls -1 / bin / usr / bin / usr / local / bin |

less

The less program is a pager, a program that shows what comes through standard page-by-page input. With the arrow keys or with space, we can go through all the information, and when we have finished examining it, just exit by pressing the q key.

But the programs not only have a standard output. They also have a standard error output. When they show an error, they usually show it by this error output. Normally it is the same terminal, and we see the error messages mixed with the program output. But we can separate it:

pi @ raspberrypi: ~ $ ls -R / etc 2> errors.txt /etc/:
adduser.conf
...
Raspberry Pi pi @: ~ $ ▂

The number 2 refers to the file descriptor corresponding to the standard error output, while the number 1 (or nothing) refers to the file descriptor of the standard output. We will talk about file descriptors when we get to the programming part of the book.

If we are only interested in errors, we can discard the standard output by redirecting it to the special file / dev / null:

pi @ raspberrypi: ~ $ ls -R / etc> / dev / null
ls: cannot open the directory / etc / polkit-1 / localauthority: Permission denied
ls: cannot open the / etc / ssl / private: Permission denied
Raspberry Pi pi @: ~ $ ▂

As a pi user, we cannot do anything. The problem with this order is that if there are many mistakes, we lose the first, which are usually the most important. Can we use a pager? No, because the pipes only connect standard output with standard input. The solution is to connect the standard error output with the same standard output, wherever you go.

pi @ raspberrypi: ~ $ ls -R / etc 2> & 1 1> / dev / null | less

Redirect descriptor 2 (standard error) to descriptor 1 (standard output), descriptor 1 (standard output) to / dev / null (discard) and connect the new standard output (new descriptor 1 which is the old error output) to the standard paginator input less.

Or without discarding the standard output, combining it together with the standard error output:

pi @ raspberrypi: ~ $ ls -R / etc 2> & 1 | less

This last form of redirection is extraordinarily useful when programming in C language. When compiling programs appear, messages from the compilation tool and also compiler errors. It is usually a lot of text, we need to see it with a pager, and we are especially interested in the first mistakes.

In addition to the pagers, it is advisable to comment in this section some filters. A filter is nothing more than a program that receives the standard input of another program, manipulates it in a certain way, and returns it to sacrifice once manipulated by the standard output.

An extraordinarily useful filter is grep (global regular expression print). It is an order that looks for lines that contain a certain pattern. Lines that do not contain the pattern are not printed, while those that contain it are printed. For example, to find all executables of / usr / bin that contain zip in the name:

pi @ raspberrypi: ~ $ ls -R / usr / bin | grep zip
Raspberry Pi pi @: ~ $ ▄

You can change the operation to print the lines that do not meet the pattern or write much more evolved patterns. When you can take some time to understand the operation of grep by reading the page of the book.

Links: In

A file has two clearly distinct parts: a name and a content. The name allows you to easily organize and find the files, but once you have found a program, you can open it (for example, with the fopen function if we are programming in C) and forget the name completely.

The idea that the name is a mere organizational device leads us to wonder if we could use several names for the same file. The answer is yes, with a link. The simplest form of link makes the source file of the destination file indistinguishable. Examine in detail this sequence of orders:

```
pi @ raspberrypi: ~ $ echo "First test"> a.txt
pi @ raspberrypi: ~ $ cat a.txt
First test
pi @ raspberrypi: ~ $ ln a.txt b.txt
pi @ raspberrypi: ~ $ echo "Second test"> b.txt
pi @ raspberrypi: ~ $ cat a.txt
Second test
Raspberry Pi pi @: ~ $ ▁
```

The ln a.txt b.txt command has created a new b.txt name for the same a.txt file. That is why when we write in b.txt, the result can also be seen in a.txt.

The problem is that this form of link does not work with folders, which are also organizational entities without other content than the names of their files. It also wouldn't work with files that are in another file system, such as a USB

skewer.
To solve these problems are the symbolic links (option -s):

pi @ raspberrypi: ~ $ ln -s src / c / reactor reactor
pi @ raspberrypi: ~ $ ls -l reactor
reactor -> src / c / reactor
Raspberry Pi pi @: ~ $ ▄

A symbolic link is simply an indication that that name really corresponds to the content labeled with another name. This solves the above problems, but the file and the link are no longer equivalent. If the file is deleted, the link hangs (dangling link), and any attempt to access will cause an error.

Symbolic links are very useful to simplify folder browsing. The last example we showed lines above is illustrative of this. If we are working with a folder continuously (reactor), it is logical to leave it more by hand in our home.

Users and Permissions

You have already noticed that as a pi user, you do not have permission to do anything. We will look in more detail at the Unix permission model and how you can skip restrictions when necessary.

The uid is the user identifier, while the gid is the group identifier. All users have a uid and a gid. However, a user can belong to many groups, as shown at the end of the id output. There is a special user, the super-user, who has the uid 0 and has no permissions limitation.

We will now examine in more detail this order ls that we saw earlier:

pi @ raspberrypi: ~ $ ls src / README.md -l

-rw-r - r-- 1 pi pi 55 Apr 11 08:26 src / README.md
Raspberry Pi pi @: ~ $ ▄

Until now, we had only seen the date and time of the last modification. However, before the date, there is much more information.

Countryside	Meaning
-rw-r - r--	Permissions
One or links)	Number of references to the file (names
Pi	User (owner)
Pi	Group (owner)
55	Size in bytes
Apr 11 08:26	Date and Time

Permissions are represented in an abbreviated notation that corresponds directly to the internal representation in the file system.

The first character represents the type of file. It is d   for directories, - for normal files, l for symbolic links, or other letters that represent other types of files (devices of various types, pipes, sockets, etc.).

The following characters are divided into three-letter groups that represent the permissions for the user who owns the file, for the group that owns the file and for everyone else, in this order. Each block of three letters represents four possible permissions, according to the following table. A script in any of the letters represents the absence of the corresponding permission.

Structure of the permissions of a file in GNU.

Excuse me		Representation
Reading	r	in the first letter
Writing	w	in the second letter

Execution	x	in the third letter
Set-id	s	in the third letter (only in user group or group)
group)		
Sticky	t	in the third letter (only in a group of others)
others)		

The read permission allows you to see the contents of the file to the corresponding group. In our example, the three groups (owner-user, owner group, and others) can read the file. That is, we can execute the cat order, or read it with an editor as Leafpad. In the case of folders, the read permission allows you to see the content, that is, do ls. Write permission allows changes to the file. In our example, only the owner pi can modify it, because none of the other permission groups have the letter w. In a folder, it means that we can add or delete items (other files or folders).

Execution permission allows you to execute the file. It is this and nothing else that makes a file executable. In GNU, there are no special extensions to identify executables. In the folders, it means that we can access what is contained in them. That implies both making a CD and accessing in any way the content of what is in the folder (see the size or owner of a file, display the content, or list a subfolder).

The set-id permission is used to set the uid or gid to the owner of the file when it is executed. That is, if an executable has the set-id permission for the owner user, then when it is executed, it does so with the permissions of that owner user (temporarily changes its uid) and not with the permissions of the user who executes it. It is a way of assigning permissions for certain operations to other users, to all who have permission to execute the file. The same can be done with the set-id permission for the owner group. When the file is executed, it does so as if the user who executed it belonged to the group that owns the file (temporarily changes its gid. This permission is normally called setuid or setgid, depending on whether it applies to the owner user or the owner group.

The sticky permission (sticky in English) has changed its meaning with the historical evolution of Unix. Nowadays, it is very useful for folders. A folder with sticky permission does not allow the files contained to be deleted or renamed by users other than the owner. It is used, for example, in the temporary folder / tmp so that some users cannot cause problems to others.

We have changed the group of the file to users, which is one of the groups to which we belong, and then we have added the write permission to the owner group. Now all users belonging to the users group can edit the archive. The order allows you to add permissions or remove them for the owner user. You can also combine both the group to which the permission applies and the permissions that apply. With -R it is applied recursively. For example:

pi @ raspberrypi: ~ $ chmod -R ug + rwX src
Raspberry Pi pi @: ~ $ ▬

Notice that the execution permit has been capitalized instead of lower case. That has a special meaning. When chmod is told X instead of x, we are telling him to only apply that permission to folders, not files.

The Super User

The super-user is the user with zero uid, which usually has the name of root. This user does not apply permission restrictions. You can do everything; you are the system administrator. Obviously, it is necessary to be an administrator to be able to do certain things, such as updating the system, installing new software, etc. But it will also be necessary to use some peripherals of the Raspberry Pi. For example, to read or change the values of the GPIO legs (General Purpose Input

Output).

In Raspberry Pi, it is considered so necessary that it is configured to be extremely simple to become superuser. Just run sudo su:

pi @ raspberrypi: ~ $ sudo su
pi @ raspberrypi: ~ # id
uid = 0 (root) gid = 0 (root) groups = 0 (root)
Raspberry Pi pi @: ~ # ▄

See how the prompt has changed. A # appears   that should be interpreted as a severe warning. Watch out!

You can destroy everything!
Try to minimize the time you are as a superuser. It is not uncommon to completely destroy the system software by mistake, and you would have to install everything from scratch.

The sudo (superuser do) order allows certain users and with certain restrictions to execute any system order as a superuser. As you can imagine is a program that has permission setuid to root. Needless run sudo su, you can run sudo, followed by anything we have to do as a superuser. For example:

pi @ raspberrypi: ~ $ sudo chown root executable
pi @ raspberrypi: ~ $ sudo chmod u + s executable
Raspberry Pi pi @: ~ $ ▄

We have changed the owner of an executable using the chown order. As superuser, we can change anything. We have put root as the new owner   (the superuser) and have added the setuid permission. This one executable moment is executed with superuser permissions.

Process Management

One of the activities that you should surely do when you are developing is to see what processes are running in the system and stop processes that may have been blocked. We will comment on only three applications for these purposes, although the range of tools is much wider. Do not stay in what we tell you, learn little by little more tools.

First of all, to see the processes that are running in the system is the order ps (processes). Without any additional argument, it provides us with information on the processes that have been executed from the same shell in which it is executed.

```
ps:
pi @ raspberrypi: ~ $ ps
PID    TTY    TIME CMD
894    pts / 0 00:00:18      bash
1211   pts / 0 00:00:00      ps
Raspberry Pi pi @: ~ $ ▄
```

In a tabular format, basic information is shown:

Countryside	Meaning
PID	Process identifier
TTY	Terminal
TIME	CPU accumulated time
CMD	Executable name

The pid (process id) is a number that assigns the operating system to all processes. Each running process must have a different pid, but once finished, its old pid can be used in another process. We can control the processes using this identification number. Let's illustrate with an example. Open a terminal and type:

pi @ raspberrypi: ~ $ cat
The cat process is waiting for data from its standard input, but we will assume that we have no idea what happens. We only know that the program does not end. We are going to kill him.

Run another terminal and type:
pi @ raspberrypi: ~ $ ps -u pi | grep cat
2093 pts / 0 00:00:00 cat
Raspberry Pi pi @: ~ $ ▄

We show all user processes pi (option -u) but then filter the output with grep to show only the lines that contain cat. The first number is the PID of the process. We will request its termination with the kill order:

pi @ raspberrypi: ~ $ kill 2093
Raspberry Pi pi @: ~ $ ▄

If you look at the first terminal, the process is over and indicates it on the screen with a message.

pi @ raspberrypi: ~ $ cat
Finished
Raspberry Pi pi @: ~ $ ▄

The program may not end. We can still do something else, and we can demand that the program end. If he doesn't do it this time, the operating system will kill him. Run cat again and in the other window:

pi @ raspberrypi: ~ $ ps -u pi | grep cat
2101 pts / 0 00:00:00 cat
pi @ raspberrypi: ~ $ kill -9 2101
Raspberry Pi pi @: ~ $ ▄

Now the message that shows the other window is slightly different:

pi @ raspberrypi: ~ $ cat
Finished
Raspberry Pi pi @: ~ $ _

The kill command is not exactly to kill processes. Actually, kill sends signals to the processes. There are a lot of signals that can be sent (use the -l option to have a list). By default, it sends signal 15 (SIGTERM) that it is a termination request. The processes can ignore it. Option -9 simply sends a different signal (SIGKILL) that processes cannot ignore.

It is also advisable to comment on the top order, which shows the state of the system in real time, putting the processes that more memory and / or CPU consume in the first place. If the system is slow and you don't know why you might have left some hanging process. Look to top what is and kill him. Once identified, you can kill it from your own top by pressing the k (kill) key. To exit press q (quit).

If the name of the executable is descriptive enough, we can kill it directly without searching for its pid using the Killall order:

pi @ raspberrypi: ~ $ killall -9 cat
Raspberry Pi pi @: ~ $ _

But keep in mind that killall sends the signal to all processes that have the CMD field like the one indicated in the argument.

Info: We propose the following exercise. Imagine that you run the file executable that you have permission setuid to root. Due to a programming error, the program does not end. What order must you execute to kill him?

Version Control

Software, like any engineering process, is an iterative process. The programs are not made at once, but gradually, adding one thing at a time. After adding a new function, it is common to perform a reengineering process, to make the whole program simpler. In this process, it is common to generate regressions; that is, things that work stop working. How do we return to the previous situation?

The solution, obviously, is managing different versions. But managing different versions manually is a tedious and error-prone process. The correct thing is to use a version control system. In this book, we propose GIT, the same one that uses the Linux kernel, and the same that we use in the documentation and in the support software of this book.

The git order is not the easiest to use program of your new Raspberry Pi, and we will not turn this book into a book about git. We will only comment on the orders you need to update the book software. That way, you will always have the latest.

The src and doc folders of your home are two GIT repositories that contain the same as in the official repositories of github.com. They were created as indicated in the appendix that describes our Raspbian customization. When a folder is a GIT repository it contains a hidden subfolder called .git

```
pi @ raspberrypi: ~ $ ls -d * /. git
doc /.git src /.git
Raspberry Pi pi @: ~ $ ▄
```

Chapter 3 - The Peripherals of the RPI

The Elements of the RPI

The Raspberry Pi has a huge number of peripherals and will not give us time to see them all. In the following sections, we will see the fundamental concepts of the majority. On the website of the book, we will be adding information that we will incorporate into future editions of this book.

Digital Inputs and Outputs

The online version of this book incorporates an interactive timeline with the history of the Raspberry Pi. Review the evolution of the Raspberry Pi concept a bit. Initially, it looked like it was going to be a USB stick, similar to the media centers that plug directly into the TV. If the goal was to reduce cost, why did it end up being much bigger?

We have to look for the answer in the objectives of the project. Its designers wanted it to be a teaching platform, not simply a cheap computer. They wanted high school students to experience for themselves not only the programming, but the construction of their own electronic equipment. It was essential that it be easy to connect things.

Therefore, from the first model, the Raspberry Pi has a good number of pins that can be configured as digital inputs or outputs to control any peripheral, sensor, or external actuator. transitions is the GPIO (General Purpose Input / Output) pins. In this chapter, we will discuss its general characteristics, and then we will see the programming details.

Comparison of the I / O Pins for the Original Models and the A + And B + Models

GPIO Connector

The original models feature a 2x13 pin connector labeled P1. All later models are compatible with these first 26 pins. This is the only one really intended to provide general purpose digital inputs and outputs. The P1 connector provides access to 17 GPIO pins. In revision 2 of the Raspberry Pi model B, next to P1 is an unpopulated socket, the 2-pin P5, which provides access to 4 additional GPIO pins.

The A + and B + models greatly extend the number of available pins from the 26-pin P1 connector to a new J8 40-pin connector. Among them, 9 more GPIO pins. However, the compatibility is total, since the first 26 pins maintain their original function.

P1 and P5 of models A and B revision 2.

Configuration of the I/O Pins in The Sockets

Digital Inputs and Outputs

From now on, we will use the numbering corresponding to the new 40-pin connector. Its equivalent in connectors P1 and P5 can be seen in the table at the beginning of this chapter. When we talk about pin numbers, we will refer to the new J8 connector unless otherwise indicated.

On the one hand, most of the pins are general purpose digital inputs / outputs. They can be configured as inputs or outputs, can be read, or written with a digital value, high or low, one or zero. Keep in mind that the high level is 3.3V, and they are not tolerant of 5V voltages.

Pins 8 and 10 can be configured as a UART interface for a conventional serial port. In fact, this is your default setting in Raspbian since the UART is used as a console.

On the other hand, pins 3 and 5 can be configured as an I2C interface to interact with peripherals that follow this protocol. In the book, we have already configured it this way. Pin 12 can be configured as PWM output. In theory, pins 12 and 13 can also be configured as an I2S (digital audio) interface, but pins are not readily available. Pins 19, 21, 23, 24 and 26 can be configured as the first interface

SPI (SPI0) to interact with peripherals that follow this protocol. In the book, we have already configured them in this way. Pins 27 and 28 are not available. They are reserved for optional incorporation of a serial memory in the expansion plates according to the HAT specification. They are the only pins that are configured as outputs at startup, and all others are initially configured as inputs to avoid problems.

Pins 29, 31, 32, 33, 35, 36, 37, 38 and 40 provide access to new GPIO legs that were not available in the original models. These legs may have other additional uses. For example, pins 32, 33, and 35 can be used for PWM outputs (only two channels available). Further, these legs complete the necessary pins to configure another SPI interface (SPI1), which we will not use in the book.

Warning

The P5 socket of the original models is originally designed to be populated from the bottom layer of the circuit. The pins in the attached figure are listed according to this criterion. If it is mounted in the upper layer, the pin assignment will be its specular reflection.
In total, we have 26 pins for digital inputs and outputs, and two of them can be used for PWM control.

GPIO Protection

When using GPIO pins for interface with hardware of any kind, care must be taken not to damage Raspberry Pi itself. It is very important to check the voltage levels and the requested current. GPIO pins can generate and consume voltages compatible with 3.3V circuits (not 5V tolerant) and can output up to 16 mA. That's enough to illuminate an LED, but for little else.

However, keep in mind that the current coming from these pins comes from the 3.3V power supply, and this source is designed for a peak load of about 3 mA for each GPIO pin. That is, even if the Broadcom SoC allows to drain up to 16 mA for each pin, the source will not be able to give more than about 78 mA in total (51 mA in the original models). There is no risk if you try to exceed this limit, but it will not work.

Warning

The GPIO pins of the Raspberry Pi are not tolerant of 5V voltages. They are intended for use with 3.3V circuits and do not have any protection. You should not drain more than 16mA per pin.

To avoid problems, a wide variety of expansion cards have been manufactured, which protect GPIO pins in various ways. The best known are:

Pi-Face Digital

Gertboard by Gert van Loo, one of the first volunteers of the Raspberry Pi Foundation. A wide variety of protection methods is available in the elinux.org tutorial titled GPIO Protection Circuits.

Program Digital Inputs and Outputs

The definitive reference for programming any of the BCM2835 peripherals is the manufacturer's data sheet, although it is a dense and arid document. The document by Gert van Loo GPIO pads control is also illustrative.

In later chapters, we will see some examples to familiarize ourselves with this peripheral, but you may want to expand the information. To begin with, probably the best tutorial is that of elinux.org, which is entitled RPi Tutorial: Easy GPIO Hardware & Software and especially programming examples using various languages and mechanisms. The Gertboard book also has abundant information, but the software is hard to find.

From the point of view of the programmer, the GPIO pins of the Raspberry Pi look like memory mapped devices. That is, to configure the pins, take digital values, or read digital signals, we have to read or write in certain memory locations. However, the Raspberry Pi processor uses a mechanism called virtual memory, in which each process sees a different address space, which does not necessarily have to correspond to the physical space, and that guarantees isolation between processes. In GNU / Linux to be able to access certain physical addresses, it is necessary to use a device (/ dev / mem) that for all purposes behaves

As a normal file. For example, in the 0x20200034 position of the device / dev / mem, the value of the GPIO0 to GPIO31 inputs can be read.

Obviously, accessing the entire physical address space is very dangerous, since it allows the entire address space of the other processes to be accessed from one process. Not only the isolation between processes is compromised, but also the security of the system. A malicious process could use privileged functions. If you think that doesn't affect you, you don't know enough about computer security. From time to time, take a look at Blackhat's presentations to see what is happening in the world of security, and you will see that it affects everything (robots, medical equipment, televisions, industrial equipment, home automation, telecommunication systems,...). A malicious user could even physically damage the Raspberry Pi. For this reason, the device / dev / mem has write permissions only for the superuser.

Recent versions of Raspbian have a / dev / gpiomem device that allows access to the GPIO pin address range only and has write permission for the gpio group. The user pi is from the gpio group. Therefore, the Pi user programs can act on GPIO pins. In practice, this may not be the case because many libraries do not yet use / dev / gpiomem.

GPIO Pin Characteristics

The GPIO pins of the Raspberry Pi incorporate a set of very interesting features:
They have the ability to limit the slew rate. This would improve noise immunity and reduce crosstalk noise, but at the cost of extending propagation times. You can program your strength drive, that is, its ability to deliver current, between 2

mA and 16 mA in 2 mA jumps (eight possible values). It basically consists of the possibility of activating more or less drivers in parallel. For more details, consult the Gert van Loo document referred to above. Normally at startup, it is set to 8 mA. This does not mean that we cannot ask for more current. Up to 16 mA is safe. However, if we exceed 8 mA, the voltage will drop to the point that a logical one can stop being interpreted as one, and the heat dissipation will be greater. On the other hand, if we program the pins to their maximum capacity, we will have current peaks that affect consumption and may affect the operation of the microSD card, especially with capacitive loads. This effect is more noticeable, the greater the number of outputs switch simultaneously.

It is possible to configure the inputs with or without Schmitt trigger so that the low- and high-level transitions have different thresholds. This allows some noise tolerance. It is possible to enable a pullup and / or pulldown resistor. Its value is around 50KOhm.

The limitation setting of slew rate, drive strength, and input with Schmitt trigger is not done pin to pin but in blocks (GPIO0-27, GPIO28-45, GPIO46-53). For the interests of the book, there should be no problems with the default configuration.

The Physical column contains the pin number on connector J8, and column V contains the read value. The Name column represents the function of the pin, but you must be careful because when GPIO appears.21, it docs not rcfcr to the Broadcom nomenclature, which is the usual one, but to a nomenclature of the WiringPi library. To interpret it correctly, you must look at the corresponding number in the BCM column, so GPIO.21 is actually GPIO 5. This artificial confusion has been the subject of numerous criticisms to the WiringPi library, but it seems that Arduino users see it as something natural.

Alternative Functions

All GPIO pins have the possibility of being used with other alternative functions. Each GPIO pin can be configured as input, output, or as one of the six alternative functions (from Alto to Alt5).

Together with your book starter kit, you will receive a card that summarizes the functions that interest us. For more details, consult the flyer that we also provide you or the elinux.org documentation that includes all the scattered information. If you do not find examples of any of the peripherals and you cannot make it work, ask in the book forum.

This scheme may be useful for advanced uses:

However, you should keep in mind that some elements cannot be selected safely because they have already been used in other parts of the Raspberry Pi. For example, the BCM2837 has two SD interfaces and two UARTs. However, both SD interfaces are busy (one for the microSD card and one for WiFi communication. Similarly, UART0 is assigned to the Bluetooth interface on the Raspberry Pi 4, and only UART1 is shown on pins 8 and 10. Another example is the clocks of general purpose (GPCLKx) that allow us to generate programmable frequency clocks on certain legs.GPCLK1 is reserved for internal use (Ethernet), and if you try to use it, most likely to hang the Raspberry Pi. Nothing serious, but not pleasant either.

Manipulating Pins in the Console

We will start using the components without writing a line of code, using programs that you have available. Connect an LED to one of the legs (for example, GPIO18) with a resistor to limit the current to 15mA. For this, you can help yourself with this table taken from theledlight.com by correcting the value for the Banggood LEDs that we have in the kit.

Kind	Drop	Resistance (15mA)
Red	1.7V	100 Ohm
Yellow	2V	87 Ohm
Green	2.1V	80 Ohm
White	2.7V	40 Ohm
Blue	2.9V	27 Ohm

The kit has a set of discrete components that includes LEDs and resistors. In theory, three of each of the colors red, yellow, green, and white are included. In practice, depending on availability, they can include other types of LEDs and even another number. For example, in a test order we made at the beginning of the year, we received 15 LEDs (5 red, 5 yellow, and 5 blue). The objectives of the book are not affected at all, so this seems a minor anecdote.

The kit LEDs are not colored, so it is difficult to know what color they are. In the bags, they usually have a letter (R, G, Y, W) to indicate the color, but not always. Anyway, if we put a resistance of 100 Ohm, we are sure not to exceed the limits, and it turns on smoothly until the blue LED. Let's see how to turn on and off the connected LED to GPIO18 leg:

```
pi @ raspberrypi: ~ $ gpio -g mode 18 out
pi @ raspberrypi: ~ $ gpio -g write 18 1
pi @ raspberrypi: ~ $ gpio -g write 18 0
Raspberry Pi pi @: ~ $ ▄
```

In the first line, we have configured the leg as output. In the following, we simply write a value on that leg (1 and 0). The -g option tells gpio to use normal leg numbering.

Note: We are in luck in the Banggood kit because white diodes have a moderate voltage drop. Unfortunately, on many other occasions, this is not the case, and it is common to have 3.4V voltage drops on a white LED. A consequence of this is that we cannot turn them on with 3.3V outputs. In those cases, you can use the level shifter or a transistor, but is it necessary? Here is the challenge, if you had a white LED with a 3.4V drop, what would you do? Use the same components as before but set the circuit to turn on without problems with a GPIO leg.

The next step is to use the GPIO legs as digital inputs. To do this, connect one of the buttons between another GPIO leg and the ground. It is also normal to put a 10K pull-up resistor between the leg and 3.3V so that the input is not floating while the button is not pressed. You can do it, but we remind you that you can also use the internal pull-up.

```
pi @ raspberrypi: ~ $ gpio -g mode 23 in
pi @ raspberrypi: ~ $ gpio -g mode 23 up
pi @ raspberrypi: ~ $ gpio -g read 23
Raspberry Pi pi @: ~ $ ▄
```

Each time we run gpio -g read 23, it will return the status (0 for the switch pressed and 1 for not pressed).

Pulse Width Modulation

Pulse Width Modulation (PWM) is a technique that consists of varying the duty cycle of a periodic digital signal, mainly with two possible objectives:

On the one hand, it can be used as a mechanism to transmit information. For example, servo motors have a digital input through which the desired angle encoded in PWM is transmitted.

On the other hand, it can be used to regulate the amount of power supplied to the load. For example, LED luminaires frequently use PWM regulators to allow intensity control.

The Raspberry Pi has several GPIO legs (GPIO12, GPIO13, GPIO18, and GPIO19) that can be configured as the output of one of the two PWM channels. BCM2835 itself is responsible for managing the signal generation, completely freeing the main processor.

The PWM peripheral of the Raspberry Pi is very flexible but only has two channels (PWM0 and PWM1). It can work in PWM mode or serializer mode. In serializer mode, simply remove the bits of the words written in a buffer in the corresponding leg. Let's look first at the PWM mode.

The user can configure two values:
- A range of values available (up to 1024).
- A value that determines the duty cycle. The PWM module is responsible for maintaining the duty cycle in the value / range ratio.

The base frequency for PWM in Raspberry Pi is 19.2Mhz. This frequency can be divided by using a divider indicated with pwmSetClock, up to a maximum of 4095. At this frequency the internal algorithm that generates the pulse sequence, but in the case of the BCM2835 there are two operating modes, a balanced mode in which it is difficult to control the width of the pulses, but allows a very high frequency PWM control, and a mark and space mode that is much more intuitive and more appropriate to control servos. The balanced mode is appropriate to control the power supplied to the load.

In mark and space mode, the PWM module will increase an internal counter until it reaches a configurable limit, the PWM range, which can be a maximum of 1024. At the beginning of the cycle, the pin will be set to 1 logical and will remain until the internal counter reaches the value set by the user. At that time, the pin will be set to 0 logical and will remain until the end of the cycle.

Let's see its application to the control of a servomotor. A servomotor has a signal input to indicate the desired inclination. Every 20ms expect a pulse, and the width of this pulse determines the inclination of the servo. Around 1.5ms is the pulse width necessary for the centered position. A smaller width rotates the servo counterclockwise (up to approximately 1ms), and a longer duration makes it rotate clockwise (up to approximately 2ms). In this case, the range and the divisor must be calculated so that the pulse is produced every 20ms, and the control of the pulse width around 1.5ms is with the maximum possible resolution.

The red servo cable (V +) is connected to + 5V in P1-2 or P1-4, the black or brown cable (V-) to GND in P1-6, and the yellow, orange, or white (signal) cable to GPIO18 on P1-12. No other components are needed.

Mounting a microservo to be controlled directly from GPIO18 configured as PWM output. To have maximum control of the servo position, we will test with the maximum range of 1024. In that case, the divisor must be such that the frequency of the PWM pulse is:

f = base
f = 19.2 × 10 6 Hz = 50 Hz
range × div
1024 × div
20 ms

That is, the splitter should be set to 390. The full range of the servo depends on the specific model. Theoretically, it should be between 52 and 102, the value being completely centered 77. In practice, the specific servo must be tested because the limits of 1ms and 2ms are not strict. Our experiments give a useful range between 29 and 123 for the TowerPro microservo available in the student kit.

Warning: Remember that there are only two PWM channels available and that these channels can only be assigned to certain legs (PWM0 in GPIO12 and GPIO18, PWM1 in GPIO13 and GPIO19).

More About PWM

For the purposes of the book, we will not stop at the PWM module, but keep in mind that the range of possibilities is much greater. We do not rule out incorporating this section in the future more information about the other modes of operation. For now, we prefer to move forward to meet other peripherals.

Keep in mind that the analog audio included in the Raspberry Pi uses the two PWM channels, so if you use analog sound, try to avoid using PWM. Our recommendation is that you use a Bluetooth speaker, or you can use an external audio board (HiFi-Berry, for example).

Configuring Raspberry Pi

To initialize our Raspberry Pi, you need to connect the peripherals you will use to the Raspberry (the essential are the SD card and the monitor); plug it in also to a power source. At startup, a screen with various information is loaded, and from there, Raspbian will be being loaded. The first time it boots up, Raspberry will display the raspiconfig tool. In case you need to run setup again, type at the command line: sudo raspi-config. Program options allow you to make the following changes:

Expand_rootfs: Allows you to expand the system of files so that you can use all of the SD card capacity.

Overscan: When a high-quality monitor is used definition, there is a possibility that the text may exceed sides of the screen, misaligning the display and losing part of the image. To correct this problem, enable the Overscan and change the values so that the image is aligned to the screen. Use positive values when the screen exit and negative values if black edges appear around it.

Configure_keyboard: The keyboard comes pre-configured with the British (UK) layout. If you want to change, select another one according to the language you will use.

Change_pass: Allows you to change the password and user.

Change_locale: Pi comes configured with the location of the United Kingdom using its style of UTF-8 encoding (en_GB.UTF-8). Select the country of your location. Example: Brazil UTF-8 (en.UTF-8).

Chang_timezone: For time zone setting, Select your region and city from your location.
Memory_split: Allows you to change the amount of memory that the GPU (graphics unit) and the CPU will use. Leave this option as default.

SSH: Allows you to enable the option to access Pi via SSH (Secure Shell) remotely over the network. Leave This option disabled allows you to save resources.

Boot Behavior: This option allows you to skip typing username and password at startup (by selecting YES). If you leave NO, you must enter these three commands (login and password can be changed in the previous option Change_pass): Raspberrypi login: pi Password: raspberry pi @ raspberrypi ~ $ startx

Update: This option allows you to update some utilities automatically, being connected to the Internet. When you have finished your settings, use the TAB key, and select Finish. It may happen that the OS restarts alone. If this does not happen and it is the first boot, type the command: pi @ raspberrypi ~ $ sudo reboot. This will force initialization with the new settings. At the desktop, we already found the Scratch programming tools and Python, in addition to the Midori browser and LXTerminal, which will be covered throughout the book.

Turning off Your Raspberry Pi (Shutting Down)

The Raspberry Pi does not have a power switch. For turn it off we should use the Logout button in the bottom corner screen right or by running the following command in shell22: pi @ raspberrypi ~ $ sudo shutdown –h now Disconnect your Pi correctly, because if pull the plug from the socket, the SD card can be corrupted and stop working.

Using Shell

Raspbian, like all Linux distribution OSs, uses the shell to execute the installation commands, modification, removal of programs, etc. The program that will be providing shell access is LXTerminal. The shell stores a command history that can be Very useful for easy typing. For example, you just need to start typing a command and hit the TAB key for the rest of the command to appear: this is very useful when you are looking for a directory. Another important facility is to be able to return the commands entered: if the execution of a command has given an error, simply press the arrow key to up, and the previous command will reappear; must then correct just the wrong part and hit enter. Previous Commands can be repeated just using the keys: up arrow, down arrow, and enter.

Let's start our programming practice. We will develop three projects with increasing levels of complexity so that you can gain expertise and develop new and increasingly sophisticated projects. You can also check out millions of examples on the Scratch website (https://scratch.mit.edu/), as well as publish your creations.

Application Development - Easy Level

Our first project, which we classify as "easy", will be called "Labyrinth". The player's goal is to pass through the maze until they reach the portal (Labyrinth Finish Line). The player also cannot circumvent the game by hacking. If he touches the wall of the maze, he must go back and choose another direction. When the actor reaches the exit, the time taken to make the route will be shown. We started by running the Scratch application, which is on the desktop. We can start by setting the stage, which will be a maze. The stage is the background where the characters move. To assemble it, you can draw the environment or import some ready-made images. To import, you can do the following:

- In the lower left corner, click on "Load Scenario Lay Programming with Raspberry Pi from File";
- In the window that opens, make the desired file path, click on it. You can also use a library image;

In this case, use the Stage icon and select one of the options presented. In our case, we will draw a maze. The ball will travel several paths within the maze and should reach the opening. To do this, go to the bottom left corner; click the Paint New Scenery icon.

In the drawing area that opens to the right, use the Rectangle and Line drawing tools and, using your creativity, draw the maze.

Do not forget that the maze must present at least one valid path that the ball must follow, starting at a starting point (in) and ending at an ending point (out). If you want to save the stage image, just go to the presentation screen and right-click, and select the "Save Picture of Stage" option. With the stage created, we can create the character that will pass through the maze; we can draw it or import it from the library, just as we did for the stage. Since we learned how to draw while setting the stage, let's now import an image from the library. To do this, go to the bottom left corner, in the Actors, New Actor area, click on the "Choose Library Actor" icon.

The library is very rich: has several character types separated by Category, Theme, and Type. Select the character you want to continue the game and click Ok. With the new Actor created, we can assign you the roles. To do this, select the actor and, in the upper strip of the screen, choose the Routes (or Scripts) option. In this tab, there is a set of commands that are separated by functions: Motion, Control, Sensors, Appearance, etc. Click the Events function, select the command When clicked, and drag it to the center of the screen: each time the "Green Flag" button is pressed, the other commands of the program will be executed.

In the following steps, we will explain the game instructions, ask the user name, create a timer, and the character control commands. Let's start by setting the character's starting position on the stage: click the Motion function, drag the Go to x: ... y: ... instruction and change the values of x and y. The x: -214 y: 160 positions correspond to the upper left side of the stage. The position of each character is always given by a pair of coordinates (x, y). To change x and y values, simply drag the object across the stage; as it is dragged, the object's coordinates (x, y) can be seen on the right of the screen. To show the game instructions, still in the Routes tab, click the Appearance function; then drag the Say statement and write the instructions to the player. To ask the player's name, click on the Sensors function and drag the Ask ... instruction and wait for the answer; you can write something else instead of what's your name?

- Click the Appearance function again and drag the Say ... statement for ... seconds;
- You can change the text Hello and the time. Again, go to the Appearance function and drag the Say ... command for ... seconds;
- Now go to the sensors function and drag the answer command into the Say ... command for ... seconds;

Through these commanders, the actor will return the name that was entered at the beginning of the game. We will again position our character to the x: -214 y: 160 position so that the player does not move the character while displaying the game instructions. At this point, the timer must be reset to start counting for a new game: click on the Sensors function and drag the Zero timer instruction.

At the end of the game, a message will appear with the elapsed time. The actor's initial positioning command should also be repeated, as the player may have moved the object while reading the instructions. The actor must be positioned at the beginning of the valid path to the maze. As a good observer, you may have already noticed that the commands are colorful and that they use them. This makes it easy to see a large script ready and to know which part of the function menu the commands were taken from.

Now let's work on the character's movements: walking will be the only action he has done. Since we want him to walk continuously until he can get out, click on his picture, then click on the Control function and drag the Always statement. Now we will define the condition for our character to move inside the stage, so go to the control function and drag the If statement;

Now we will define which key will move the character right, left, up, and down. Go to the Sensors function and choose the instruction key ... pressed and choose the key that will use to move your character to the left side; we use the left arrow key. With our first side defined, we will say which direction belongs on the left side. Go to the Motion function and drag the instruction point to the direction and position the direction that belongs to the left side, in this case - 90 degrees. Select the Routes tab again, click on the Motion function; drag the Move ... steps instruction into the always opening;

In this command, we define that the character will walk when we press one of the arrows; type 5 in the number of steps. Repeat for the remaining three directions. To advance the process and not have to type the entire command again by hand, go to the first code and click the right button and choose the duplicate option so you can duplicate the code and change it without having to rewrite the code.

When the character touches the walls of the maze, he must return (the player cannot cheat through a wall). For this, we need to use decision and repeat commands: when touching the maze line, he must go back 5 steps to be within the allowed limits. To use decision commands, click the Sensors function and drag the instruction Tapping color ...?;

Then click on the color box and select the desired color from the color box that appears. The mouse cursor will cause the color box to change according to the color it passes over. Now let's create the maze output:

- We draw a portal;
- When the cat touches him, the game will be over, and the victory song will be played.

The portal must be an actor. Since we already imported an actor from the library, in this case, we will draw him. In the lower left corner of the screen, under Actors, New Actor, click Paint New Actor (Brush icon). Now use your creativity and draw the portal. With the portal created, let's put its functions. The new actor's first command is the same as that used for the first actor: clicking on the green start flag (Events) and positioning yourself (Movement); The portal should be positioned in the final exit position of the maze. The next command will be Control (the Always Repeat). The next command defines the end of the game: every time our character (Cat) touches the Portal, the message of victory will be given, the time with which the course was made, and a song will be played. Try to complete the script: the commands exit the Events, Motion, Control, Sensors, Sound, Appearance, and Control again.

We have already seen that we can put sounds in the project: from the library, importing a sound of our own or recording a sound. We even saw that we have resources to edit the sounds that we will use. Let's put the sound in our project by importing it from the library. Select the Sound function and drag the Play Sound ... command. Now click on the Sounds tab; then click on the Upload sound from file icon, scroll to the Scratch library path and select the Congratulations sound. This concludes the first project. Note the start and end points. To play, click on the green flag and use the arrow keys to command the character.

Application Development - Middle Level

Now let's create a Ping Pong game to play in pairs, which we can consider at an intermediate level. This project is very interesting because it works with practically all functions of the Scratch platform. The goal of the game is also simple: whoever can play the ball beyond the opponent's racket score points; who can make 5 points, is the winner. First, let's create the stage: it will have two lines behind the rackets, representing the limit to how far the ball will reach; whenever the ball touches these lines, the point will be the opponents. Following the script and draw the stage. The red and blue colors are important as they will be used as a control to score points for each player. The ball to use in the game is an actor; let's import it from the library. Now let's create the rackets;

Just create one and then duplicate it. Go to the Actors area (bottom left) and click the Paint New Actor (brush) icon. To duplicate the racket, in the Actors area, right-click it; in the popup menu, click Duplicate. The duplicate option creates a new character in the Actor area. The second racket will have no link to the first racket. Drag the rackets and scoreboard (Player 1 Player 2 variables) across the stage. Once the stage and the characters are created, we will program the ball and then the balls and rackets. At the beginning of the game, the ball should be in the center of the stage. Enter the commands:

When you click and Go to x: ... and y: ... and type 0 for x and y. Then drag the Point instruction to the direction 90 degrees (from the Motion function); click on the box to enter the degrees (90) and within that command, go to the Operators function and drag the command Choose a number between 1 and 10; enter 180 instead of 10. Now let's set the score for two players (there will be two variables). To do this, select the Variables function, click Create a variable, and type Player 1; do the same for Player 2. Remember that variables will only be created for the ping pong ball, they will serve as a counter for the game score. Leave the two checkboxes next to the variables checked so that they appear on the Stage; drag them on the Stage to place them in the position you want.

The two variables (representing each player's score) must start the game with zero. To do so, double-drag the command change Player to 0 for the script; change the first instruction to Player 1 and to 0 (zero); change the second statement to Player 2 and to 0 (zero). Also, drag the instruction wait 1 sec from the Control function and change the time to 1.5 seconds.

Score Counting Variables

The game should last until one of the players (Player 1 or Player2) reaches 5 points. To do this, drag the command Repeat until it is in the Control functions. There is a hexagon after the until: drag the operator or to the hex (also from the Control function); now, we have two hexagons.

Drag the = operator to the first hexagon. To the first box of or drag Player 1 (from the Variables function); in the second box, type 5. Repeat for Player 2: drag the = operator to the second hex; to the first box or drag Player 2 (from the Variables function); In the second box, type 5.

Decision Commands

Within the Command, repeat until most of the project logic occurs. The ball should come back every time it touches the edge;

If we do not put this command, the ball will be stuck on the edge without returning to the game. To do this, drag to the opening of Repeat until the command. If you touch the edge, come back (from the Motion function): this is a decision command that performs a single statement: back. The following instruction Move 7 steps (also from the Motion function) will always be executed even if the ball does not touch the border. Drag the If ... Then statement (from the

Control function); drag the instruction Touching color? to the hexagon; put the black color in the box. To select the color inside the canister, click on the color inside the canister and drag the mouse to the black color. Touching the black color, the ball should come back. To program this, do the following: drag the Point instruction to the direction ... degrees (Motion function); then drag the minus operator (Operators function) to the ellipse with the degree value (we now have two ellipses to fill in); to the first ellipse, drag the direction instruction (from the Motion function); at the second ellipse type 180. We want the ball to make a random move on the way back so that its trajectory becomes unpredictable, and the game gets busier. Drag the instruction rotate ... degrees (from the Motion function); then drag the Pick number operator between ... and ... (from the Operators function); type - 20 in the first ellipse and 20 in the second. Next, we want the ball to move in that direction: drag the Move ... steps instruction (Motion function) and type 10 in the ellipse. If the ball touches the edge of the stage, we should score the opponent and return the ball to the center of the stage.

To do this, drag the If ... Then and Tapping Color ... commands; put the color blue. This command should be just below the Se, still inside Repeat until. Now drag the Add to ... statement (from the Variables function) into the opening of the If ... then; select Player 1 for the variable to add. Drag instruction Wait ... sec (Control function); type 2 for seconds. Drag Go to x: ... y: ... (Motion function) and type 0 for both. The instructions for counting Player 2 are almost identical. Repeat, therefore, the steps of the previous paragraph, changing only the player and the color. When either Player 1 or Player 2 reaches 5 points, the program will exit the Repeat command until that is what this command controls. Then we need to see who made the 5 points. To do so, drag another If ... statement then ... (from the Control function) to after the Repeat command until. Drag to the hexagon of If ... the operator = (from the Operators function); to the first box do = drag Player 1 (from the Variables function); in the second box, type 5. Now drag to the first opening of the Se ... then, otherwise ... the Say ... statement for ... seconds; type in "Player 1 Champion !!!" and 2 in the seconds box.

Right-click this instruction, and on the popup menu, click Duplicate. Drag the duplicate statement to the Snag opening and click again to drop the copied statement; type "Player 2" in place of "Player 1". These are the commands defined for the ball actor. Since we have three actors on stage (the ball and two rackets), we need to write the racket scripts. Rackets can only move up and down. The first will use the W keys to go up and S to go down; the second will use the up arrow and down arrow keys. We need two command blocks for each racket. Have you seen the commands When you click and Go to x: ... y: ... and the Always command. The command set then programs the racket to go up when you press the W key. To the hexagon drag the Command key ... pressed (from the Sensors function) and select W to the key;

inside the opening of If ... then two instructions will enter: Add ... ay (from the Motion function) and another If ... then. Enter 15 in the first statement;

This changes the position of the racket, causing it to rise as it increases the value of its y coordinate. As the racket went up, the following statement

If ... then checks if it touched the edge: drag the Tapping ... command? (from the Sensors function) to the hexagon and select edge. Drag another instruction Go to x: ... and y: ... to the second If ... then type - 42 and 11. The other instruction set programs the racket to come down when you press the S key. and check if it touched the bottom edge. You can duplicate the whole set: right-click the If ... statement and then Duplicate. Drag the duplicate statement below If ..., then still inside Always, and click to drop it. Make the appropriate changes: Select Y instead of W; enter -15 in place 15; type -293 instead of 11. Note that by keeping the x value constant at -42 and varying y, the racket only moves vertically (up and down). For Player 2, the only changes are: Up Arrow and Down Arrow keys and racket x and y positions. Since the instruction group looks similar, you can duplicate it.

Right-click the instruction. When you click ... and select Duplicate: The entire group of "docked" statements will be duplicated. Drag the instruction group into the Actors area and click to drop it onto actor Racket 2. Now click on actor Racket 2 to have its script (the duplicate) shown. Change the keys and x and y positions.

Application Development - Hard Level

Let's now create a difficult level game that we will call Block Breaker: The Game will have a Menu, game over screen and will be controlled by the mouse. The interesting thing about the block breaking game is that it works with practically all the functions found on the Scratch platform and the player will have a lot of fun developing the game and playing, as the main objective of the game is to be able to break all the blocks in the shortest time.

Let's import the library stage: go to the bottom left corner and click on the Choose background icon;

Several models of the library are shown, choose one (this may be Brick wall 1) and click Ok. Using Paint Editor (see item PAINT EDITOR) draw a green line at the bottom of the wall;

Note that there is a scroll bar under the stage;

Remember to draw the line along its full length.

This line will be the limit: every time the ball touches it, thus passing through the racket, a message of Game Over will be sent, and the game will end. Now let's create the racket (our first actor) that will hit the ball to break the blocks. Repeat what you have already done; the racket is now horizontal and blue. The blocks that will be destroyed by the ball are also actors. Just as you did with the racket, draw a block. Duplicate the blocks (in our case, we get 18 blocks). Name the blocks by numbering them: Block 1, Block 2, Block 3 ... and set the colors for the blocks to have a heterogeneous structure. Our other actor is the ball; let's import it from the library. After creating all the actors, drag them on the stage. Now we need to program each of these characters. The first script will be the racket: it will only walk on the x axis, following the mouse, and should hit the ball. Click on the Actor Racket, and on the Scripts, tab enter the two start instructions. When you click and Go to x: ... and y: ...; change the starting position to x: -58 and yy: -148. Then enter the Always statement.

Drag the Change x statement to ... (from the Motion function) to the Always open; then drag the Mouse Position x instruction (from the Sensors function) to the typing box. This will keep the racket on the same line (y axis) but will follow the mouse to the right and left (varying the x axis). This is just the racket script. The blocks also have a simple behavior: when the game starts, they show themselves in a certain position; if they are touched by the ball, they hide.

To do this, we will use two new commands: Show and Hide (from the Appearance function). Click on a block to start your script. Put the command When you click ... (from the Events function), then drag the Show (from the Appearance function) command and the Go to x: ... y: ... (from the Motion function) and type -186 and 176. Enter the Always statement (from the Control function) and drag, within its opening, an If ... Then statement (from the Control function); drag the instruction Tapping ...? (from the Sensors function) after Se ... and select Ball from the selection box. Inside If ... then, enter two commands: Wait ... sec (from the Control function) and Hide (from the Appearance function); enter 0.2 for seconds (duplicate the script for each block and change only the position of each).

Now let's develop the functions of the main character, the little ball. In addition to moving in any direction, the ball will also control the player's score: every time he destroys one of the blocks, it will add a point for the player. Click on the ball, in the Actors area, and on Scripts. Enter the command When you click ... (from the Events function) and o Go to x: ... y: ... (from the Motion function) and type -26 and 67. That way, the ball will be above the racket. Drag the Point statement to the direction ... degrees (from the Motion function) and select o for the degrees; This direction makes the ball go up. In the Variables function, create a variable named Score. Drag the Change ... to ... instruction to get the score to start with zero. The game ends in three situations: if all blocks are destroyed, time is up, or if the ball touches the green line. Let's put the Always loop function; within the opening of this command. The next other command blocks will always come. Drag both instructions Move ... steps, and If you touch the border, go back (from the Motion function); This sets the speed of the ball and keeps it within the edges of the stage.

The next block will add 1 point to the scoreboard if a block is destroyed; It will take a little work because there are so many blocks. Drag the If ... Then command (from the Control function). Drag the Raspberry Pi 111 Or operator (from the Operators function) to the hex after the If. now drag to the first hex of the instruction Tapping ...? (from the Sensors function) and select Block 1. Now you need to test the other blocks. To the empty hex of the Or drag another operator Or; to the first empty hexagon drag another instruction Tapping ...? and select Block 2. To empty Or's hexagon drag another Or operator; to the first empty hexagon drag another instruction Tapping ...? and select Block 3. Since we have 18 blocks, you should repeat this process for the first 17 blocks. The last operator Or will receive in each hexagon a Tapping ...? Instruction, one for Block 17 and one for Block 18. Then we will put three commands, which will be executed when a block is destroyed: add 1 point on the scoreboard, turn the ball back and play a song. Drag the Add to ... 1 statement from the Variables function; select Score. Drag the Point statement to the direction ... degrees; complete it by placing an operator less the same as you did previously. Drag the Play Sound ... statement from the Sound function and import a song from the library.

When the ball touches the racket, it must change direction and make a random movement; We have already done this with the ping pong ball. Drag another statement If ... then; then drag the Tapping ... statement to the If hex. (from the Sensors function) and select Racket. Drag into the If ... then the Point to direction ... degrees direction; complete it by placing an operator less the same as you did; Now, however, the subtraction is reversed. Then drag the Rotate ... degrees instruction (from the Motion function) and complete it. If the ball passes the racket and touches the green line, the game ends, and the player's score is shown. You have already used them all: If ... then, with Tapping color ... Say ... for ... seconds and Stop. If the score reaches the maximum, we display the Congratulations message and the score obtained by the player. You have already used them all: If ... then; the others can be duplicated. We still have to watch the timer: let's limit the playing time to two minutes; if it exceeds, Game over! Drag another function If ... then (from the Control function); drag to hex after the If Greater operator> (from the Operators function); now drag to the first hex of the> Timer Value (from the Sensors function) statement; type 120 in the second hex of>. Duplicate the two instructions Say ... for ... seconds and Stop ... and place them inside the Se ... opening then.

Chapter 4 - I2C Communications

The Raspberry Pi has two peripherals to implement I2C, the BSC (Broadcom Serial Controller) that implements the master mode, and the BSI (Broadcom Serial Interface) that implements the slave mode. We will describe only the BSC, which has much greater interest for this book.

The BSC implements three independent masters that have to be on separate I2C buses (does not allow multi-master). However, BSC0 is reserved for the identification of expansion plates (HAT specification, pins 27 and 28), and BSC2 is exclusively for the HDMI interface. We will, therefore, usually use BSC1, using pins 3 and 5 of connector J8.

The programming interface is, as in all Raspberry Pi peripherals, a set of memory mapped records. However, in this case, there is an operating system kernel driver that significantly simplifies life.

Explore the Bus

Devices connected to an I2C bus have a 7-bit address. Although there is the possibility of using 10-bit addresses, the truth is that it is quite rare to find devices with addresses of more than 7 bits. In this book, we will assume 7-bit addresses. This implies that at most, we can have 117 devices connected (some addresses are reserved).

The first thing we can do is discover what I2C interfaces we have available. In the original models, only BSC0 was available, while in the new BS0, it is used for the identification of HAT (hardware attached on top) expansion boards. You can examine it yourself by running i2cdetect:

pi @ raspberrypi: ~ $ i2cdetect -l

I2C-1 I2C 3f804000.i2c I2C adapter Raspberry Pi pi @: ~ $ ▄
Only one I2C interface (i2c-1) appears. Now we can look at what devices are connected on the bus. Connect the MPU6050 module that is included in the kit. Just connect GND, VCC to 3.3V, SDA, and SCL. We will use i2cdetect again, indicating now the available I2C bus number:

```
pi @ raspberrypi: ~ $ i2cdetect -y 1
        012345678        9 a b c d e f
00:     - - - - - -       - - - - - - -
10:     - - - - - - - - -     - - - - - - -
twenty: - - - - - - - - -     - - - - - - -
30:     - - - - - - - - -     - - - - - - -
40:     - - - - - - - - -     - - - - - - -
fifty:  - - - - - - - - -     - - - - - - -
60:     - - - - - - - - 68    - - - - - - -
70: - - - - - - - -
```
Raspberry Pi pi @: ~ $ ▄

Only one device connected with address 68 is displayed in hexadecimal (0x68). Actually, the MPU6050 can have two addresses setting the leg AD0. Normally that little leg has a pull-down that sets it to logical zero, which corresponds to the address 0x68, but we can connect it to 3.3V to have the address 0x69. This allows to have two MPU6050 on the same bus. One with address 0x68 and one with address 0x9.

We can now read and write on any of the connected I2C devices.

We have read register 117 of the device with address 0x68 of the bus i2c -1. The MPU6050 is an accelerometer and gyroscope of InvenSense also measures temperature and can be combined directly with a magnetometer to have an IMU (Inertial Measurement Unit) complete.

If we look at the map of records, record 117 corresponds to Who Am I., and it is a record that simply returns the base address of the device. It can be used to make sure the device is in the expected direction and is responding. It is a read-only record, so if we try to write on, it will ignore it completely.

Let's read the last temperature measurement. The measurement is in registers 65 and 66, but if we read the two registers independently, we can be reading part of the temperature of one measurement and another part of another measurement. That is why you have to read the two records at once, making a 16-bit transfer (word mode):

```
pi @ raspberrypi: ~ $ i2cget -y 1 0x68 65 w
0x0000
Raspberry Pi pi @: ~ $ ▄
```

Oops, a strange value. Something fails. It is normal to take a little time to carefully read the data sheet and the map of records to understand how it works. The clue to the problem comes to us as soon as we try to read record 107 (Power Management 1):

```
pi @ raspberrypi: ~ $ i2cget -and 1 0x68 107
0x40
Raspberry Pi pi @: ~ $ ▄
```

That means that bit 6 is set to one, which curiously corresponds to the SLEEP mode. The device starts in sleep mode to not consume battery, and we have to wake it up by removing that bit.
This is something else. We already have temperature readings. But it is very important to interpret them well. I2C is a byte-oriented protocol. It is transferred byte to byte. When transferring a word through I2C, the computer understands that the low byte first arrives and then the high one. This

agreement is called little-endian and is the dominant one today. However, if we look at the map of records, we will see that address 65 corresponds to the high byte and 66 to the low byte. Therefore, the bytes are changed! The reading must be interpreted as 0xf290. Let's see how we can do it with the shell:

```
pi @ raspberrypi: ~ $ T = $ (i2cget -y 1 0x68 65 w)
pi @ raspberrypi: ~ $ echo "0x $ {T: 4: 2} $ {T: 2: 2}"
0xf230
Raspberry Pi pi @: ~ $ ▄
```

Whatever the order takes, we put it in a variable, and then we print it, followed by the two characters. It's time to think about doing a program in C or Python. But even if it is to leave the full example, we will make the complete transformation at a temperature in degrees Celsius:

```
pi @ raspberrypi: ~ $ echo "$ (($ T - 0x10000)) / 340 + 36.53" | bc -l 26.13000000000000000000
Raspberry Pi pi @: ~ $ ▄
```

We make up the formula that comes in the map of records. The temperature is the value of the record correctly interpreted match by 340 plus 36.5. The problem is that the shell does not know how to do arithmetic operations with real ones, so we leave it to another program, in this case, bc. To bc, we pass the expression to be calculated, which is 0xf230 / 340 + 36.5. The problem is that bc does not understand hexadecimal numbers, so we have to pass it to signed decimal. This can be done with the $ ((x)) operator of the shell, which is used to calculate simple operations with integers. As it is negative, its value is the result of subtracting 0x10000.

Too complicated? Yes, I think so too. That is why we need to simplify this with the most powerful mechanism offered by computer science: abstraction. But we will leave this by the time we see how to implement all these readings in C or Python.

The i2cdump command allows a set of records to be read in a burst. We read at once from register 61 to 72. They correspond to the readings of (in order):

Accelerometer:
Acceleration in X: 0xfdf4
Acceleration in Y: 0xfe5c
Acceleration in Z: 0x3ef0
Temperature: 0xf160.
Gyroscope:
X rotation: 0xffa2
Y rotation: 0xff39
Z rotation: 0xff78

It only remains to interpret these numbers as signed integers in addition to 2. It is proposed as an exercise.

The gyroscope measures the speed of rotation in the three axes. Obviously, if a global reference is not available, error will accumulate, and its absolute measurement will not be very useful in determining the actual orientation. That is why the MPU6050 has the option of coupling with a magnetometer, which provides a real reference of the north, which allows for correcting the accumulated errors. In the book, we will not use magnetometer, but consider it for your projects.

Chapter 5 - SPI Communications

SPI is an alternative protocol to I2C that many devices use. Today it is common to find devices that implement both I2C and SPI. The choice of which one to use depends on the application:

- I2C uses fewer pins and allows to address many more devices.
- SPI uses more pins but allows much faster speed.

Like I2C, it is a serial protocol, but the address of the devices is not transmitted through the data channel, but specific legs are used to select them. As in I2C, there is a teacher who takes the active role in communication and one or several slaves who assume the passive role.

Home SPI interface has at least four legs:

- SCLK (Serial CLocK). Clock signal with respect to which the rest of the signals are synchronized.
- MISO (Master In, Slave Out). Data input for the master, data output for the slave.
- MOSI (Master Out, Slave In). Data output for the master, data input for the slave.
- CEn (Chip Enable). One or more target selection signals active at low level. To send or receive from the zero device, the signal CE0 is activated, for the device, one CE1 is activated, etc.

In the Raspberry Pi, we have three independent peripherals to implement the slave and master mode. The slave mode incorporates it into the same BSI (Broadcom Serial Interface) that also implements the I2C slave. In the book, we will see the master mode, which has much more practical interest.

The Raspberry Pi has three SPI master interfaces (SPI0, SPI1 and SPI2) although only one of them (SPI0) is visible for the original models and two of them (SPI0 and SPI1) for the models with J8 40-pin connector. Each of these interfaces has two destination selection lines (CE0 and CE1). SPI0 is more evolved since it allows DMA (direct memory access). SPI0 is designed for high-speed transfers (clock up to 125Mhz) without producing a significant load for the processor. However, SPI1 has no possibility of using DMA and only has a small four-bit 32-bit FIFO.

The student kit has an analog-digital converter with SPI interface CJMCU-1118, which incorporates the Texas Instruments ADS1118. It is a 16-bit analog-digital converter with programmable gain amplifier and with a temperature sensor. It can measure four analog signals referred to ground or two differential analog signals. We will illustrate the use of SPI with this module.

To do this, we will have to study your data sheet well before working with it. For now, to familiarize ourselves with the device, we will connect a 10K potentiometer.

Mounting a 10KOhm potentiometer as an analog source for the CJMCU-1118. To communicate with an SPI device, we must first configure a series of parameters:

The polarity of the chip select signal (CSPOL). It is normally active at a low level and does not need to be modified.

The polarity of the clock (CPOL). A value of 0 means that the rest level of the clock is low. A value of 1 means that the rest level of the clock is high.

The reloj phase (CPHA). If it has a value of 0, it means that SCLK transitions occur in half of every bit of data transmitted. A value of 1 means that SCLK transitions occur at the beginning of each bit.

Clock frequency. It is configured by selecting a clock source and a divider (CDIV). The clock source is usually 125MHz. The different combinations of CPOL and CPHA give rise to the four possible modes:

Mode	CPOL	CPHA
0	0	0
1	0	1
2	1	0
3	1	1

From the ADS1118 data sheet, we can see that the device is compatible with mode 1 (CPOL = 0, CPHA = 1). The CE polarity is also active low and supports a clock of up to 4MHz. To interact with it, we will use the tools included in the pigpio library. In particular, we will use pigpiod and its interface of pigs orders. First, we run the pigpiod server:

pi @ raspberrypi: ~ $ sudo pigpiod
Raspberry Pi pi @: ~ $ ▄

We use sudo to run with superuser permissions. It is called a server because it handles client requests. By itself, it does nothing but waits for a client to request specific operations. The client is called pigs and can run as a normal user. For example:

pi @ raspberrypi: ~ $ pigs help

...
Raspberry Pi pi @: ~ $ ▄

Countryside	Meaning
mm	SPI mode
ppp	CEi polarity. 0 = active low, 1 = active high.
uuu	Use of CEi. 0 = used, 1 = not used.
TO	Auxiliary SPI. 0 = normal SPI, 1 = auxiliary SPI.
W	Number of cables 0 = 4 wires (normal), 1 = 3 wires.
nnnn	Number of bytes to write before changing MOSI to MISO (only for W = 1).
T	Order of transmitted bits. 0 = MSb first, 1 = LSb first.
R	Order of bits received. 0 = MSb first, 1 = LSb first.
bbbbbb	Word size in bits (0-32). 0 = 8 bits. Only for auxiliary SPI.

We are lucky because most of the default parameters correspond to the values that the CJMCU-1118 module needs. Just change the SPI mode.

pi @ raspberrypi: ~ $ pigs spio 0 4000000 10
Raspberry Pi pi @: ~ $ ▄

Now, we have to configure the module with the inputs referred to ground, in continuous mode at 128 SPS and with measuring range (FSR) of ± 2,048V. The ADS1118 writes your configuration while reading data. If you don't want to write the configuration log, you just have to write zeros.

With the printf program, we can print values in a similar way to the printf C function. The $ (order) operator of the shell simply returns the standard output of the order it encloses. In this case, we use it to put the sample in hexadecimal in the variable V. We then use the operator $ ((expr)) of the shell to transform that hexadecimal number into decimal, and we compose an expression that is calculated by bc.

Chapter 6 - UART Communication

UART stands for Universal Asynchronous Receiver Transmitter. It is the dominant serial communication interface in low-end microcontrollers and old computers. Before USB, the UART was the mechanism to connect the keyboard, the mouse, or even the communications modem. Before, it was still the interface used by terminals or consoles to interact with a computer. The Terminal program that you run on your Raspberry Pi is nothing but an emulation of these old terminals.

Nowadays, it is almost impossible to find one of these serial interfaces on a computer, and it has been practically replaced by USB. Fortunately, we have special USB cables that incorporate a UART-USB adapter. In the student kit of this book, you have one. This adapter allows you to communicate the UART of the Raspberry Pi with any USB port, either from a computer or another Raspberry Pi. This allows you to use the Raspberry Pi without having a monitor and without having a network connection or USB keyboard. For example, from another Raspberry Pi or from a laptop.

The serial port occupies the GPIO14 (TxD) and GPIO15 (RxD) pins. By default, Raspbian uses these pins for a serial console. The Broadcom SoC supports two UARTs, but both are configured on the same pins of the J8 header. UART0 is a standard ARM peripheral (PL011) and implements all expected capabilities in a high performance UART. UART1 implements a simplified version that is called mini-UART by the manufacturer. It is intended to be used with low transfer rate devices, such as the console.

In all Raspberry Pi models except in the Compute Module, we only have GPIO14 and GPIO15 pins for both UARTs. For this reason, Raspbian uses UART0 for the console, and UART1 is not usually used.

But of course, that means the UART is busy on the console. It is necessary to remove the console in order to use the UART for other purposes. To disable the console, you have to edit the file /boot/cmdline.txt as superuser, delete the fragment that says console = serial0,115200, and restart the Raspberry Pi.

To use the GPIO14 and GPIO15 pins as digital input / output pins, use the configuration tool and, in the Interfaces, tab deactivate the Serial option.
But let's go back to its use as a console, which is very useful when you want to put your Raspberry Pi in a robot or other equipment where plugging a monitor is unthinkable. It is possible to connect a USB cable to these pins to connect to the Raspberry Pi without the need for any network configuration. In the student kit, you will have received a USB cable on one end and with four female Dupont connectors on the other. You can connect it in the following way:
The red wire is the USB power (5V). The Raspberry Pi already has its own power, so you must connect it again. The black wire is the ground, connect it to pin J8-6. The white cable is the data transmission from the UART to the USB port. Connect it to pin J8-8 (GPIO14).

The green cable is the one to receive data from the USB port to the UART. Connect it to pin J8-10 (GPIO15).

This should be enough to have the console running on any Raspberry Pi model before 3B. The problem is that in the Raspberry Pi 4, the UART is used for the Bluetooth interface, and the console is configured with the mini-UART. This has important consequences that are not entirely resolved yet. As a user, you are not going to face the problems it poses at all, but keep in mind that for the mini-UART to work correctly, you have to set the core frequency to 250 MHz; it is not possible to modulate the frequency to save consumption.

Testing the console is very simple, using Raspberry Pi itself. Also, connect the USB end of the cable to a free USB port and run:

pi @ raspberrypi: ~ $ miniterm.py / dev / ttyUSB0 115200
Raspbian GNU / Linux 8 raspberrypi ttyS0
raspberrypi login:

Enter as pi user and raspberry password. As you can see, you have a fully functional console in the UART. You can connect to it with any laptop and use the Raspberry Pi without the need for a monitor and keyboard.

For mobile devices, it is a great advantage. To exit miniterm.py, press the Ctrl, AltGr, and] key.

It is beyond the objectives of the book to explain how to use the console from a Windows laptop. If you have a GNU / Linux on your laptop, the system is the same, as we have explained. Install the screen tool and use it the same as we have used miniterm.py. In that case, you get out with Ctrl-A followed by \.

Chapter 7 - Network Communications

The most used Raspberry Pi models (B, B +, 2B, and 3B) incorporate an Ethernet interface. The new 3B model also incorporates a WiFi interface, and most users of other models use a USB WiFi skewer (WiFi dongle) to update the system. Therefore, it is obligatory that we speak a little of communications, although we will do it from a purely practical perspective, without going into excessively technical details. Of course, we recommend that you expand the information with the extensive literature available.

Communication networks today use the family of TCP / IP protocols for the most part. These are the protocols that were designed to build the Internet, the network of networks. There are two versions currently in use IPv4 (Internet Protocol v4) and IPv6. Although they are quite similar, there are important differences that mostly escape the interest and scope of this book. We will see enough of IPv4 to handle our communication needs between devices and leave IPv6 for future editions when their degree of adoption is higher.

The TCP / IP family of protocols is primarily built on the IP protocol, which provides basic capabilities and guarantees. These include addressing and routing.

IPv4 Addresses

Each network interface can have several IP addresses, and we can manage them if we want to manually. IP addresses basically work as postal codes. They are organized hierarchically, which facilitates delivery. For example, if we send a letter to the 45005 zip code, the mailman knows it is from Toledo because it starts with 45. Therefore, it will arrive first at the Toledo post office, which in turn will distribute it to its different provincial delegations. On the Internet, each post office is called a router, and the IP addresses, unlike postal codes, fully identify the recipient computer.

But how do messages get to a computer? A network interface is clearly needed. Therefore, the addresses are associated with that network interface. It can be understood as a door of a house. The mailman leaves the letter at a door, but nothing prevents a house from having more than one door. Each door has a different address (number) associated.

Let's examine a little the network of my own Raspberry Pi, and then we will see how to configure yours. We are interested in the last part of the output of the ip addr command, which can also be achieved like this:

pi @ raspberrypi: ~ $ ip addr list wlan0

3: wlan0: < BROADCAST, MULTICAST, UP, LOWER_UP > mtu 1500 qdisc mq state UP group default qlen 1000 link / ether 00: 13: ef: 71: 03: d0 brd ff: ff: ff: ff: ff: ff inet 192.168.1.38/24 brd 192.168.1.255 global scope wlan0 valid_lft forever preferred_lft forever inet6 fe80:: 146d: 4f11: 30bf: 17a4 / 64 scope link valid_lft forever preferred_lft forever
Raspberry Pi pi @: ~ $ ∎

Three address lists appear: link / ether correspond to what is known as link level addresses. It is a very important technical term, but that we will not see in the book. The inet tag corresponds to the IPv4 data, which we will use in the book. The inet6 tag corresponds to the IPv6 data that we will leave for future extensions. Let's stop on the IPv4 data.

The IP address (e.g., 192.168.1.38) is a sequence of 4 octets (numbers 0 to 255), usually separated by periods. The suffix / 24 serves to indicate which part of the address (in bits counted from the most significant) is common to all the subnet and what part is specific to each computer in the subnet. With the metaphor of the mail, it would be equivalent to determining which part of the address is the name of the street and which part is the house number. In our case, 192.168.1 is common for the entire network, and only the last number is indicative of the computer.

The scope or scope of the address indicates in which contexts that address makes sense. The interesting addresses have global reach, allow to communicate to the computer with any of those connected to the entire Internet. Other addresses will have host scope, as with the lo interface. These addresses are not intended to communicate processes beyond your computer, and it would be a mistake to pretend to use it to communicate two different computers.

Name Service

And it doesn't surprise you that after all these years using the Internet you never had to use IP addresses? Well, maybe in the configuration of the WiFi hotspot, or to share files between mobiles, but little else. I'm wrong?

The reason is that this address mechanism is simplified with another additional protocol, the name service (DNS, Domain Name System). It is a service similar to the yellow pages of the phones. We don't have to know or remember all the phones; we just have to look for the name in the phone book. The DNS works similarly.

Transport Protocols

A communications network is here to communicate, so let's do it. In this chapter, we will only use tools from your Raspberry

Pi without typing a single line of programs. We will start with netcat, a wonderful tool to test network programs. Open two different terminals and execute the following in the first one:

pi @ raspberrypi: ~ $ nc -l 8888

The program waits (option l means listen, listen) without doing anything. It is what is known as a server. Go to the other terminal and execute the following.

pi @ raspberrypi: ~ $ nc 127.0.0.1 8888

Message Test

This time we run netcat as a client connected to address 127.0.0.1. That is the address of the loopback interface, so we connect to our own computer. Look in the first terminal. Magic! Type now in the first terminal:

pi @ raspberrypi: ~ $ nc -l 8888
Message Test

Another Message Test

It looks like that? You have a bidirectional data channel. You can send and receive interchangeably. To exit press the key Ctrl and without releasing press the letter C.

The number 8888 is what is known as a port number. If we continue with the post metaphor, it would be equivalent to the mailbox inside an apartment house. A port is reserved for each service. Ports below 1024 are privileged in the sense that they are used for system services and therefore a normal user cannot handle requests on those ports. Let's look at an example, port 80 is the web server port. Run this:

pi @ raspberrypi: ~ $ sudo ip addr add 161.67.137.169 dev lo

```
pi @ raspberrypi: ~ $ sudo nc -l 80 << EOF
HTTP / 1.0 200 OK
< html > < body > < h1 > You fool! </ h1 > </ body > </ html
>
```

EOF

Now run the web browser and try to view the page www.uclm.es. Surprised?

We have added an IP address to the interface loopback that matches that of www.uclm.es. When we enter this site in the browser, it uses the DNS to obtain the corresponding IP address and sends a request message to that IP address. As it is a known IP address, the message does not even leave the computer; it remains the loopback interface. In all directions of the computer, we have netcat listening on port 80, so that message request comes to netcat. What is between and EOF is just a way of indicating that this is what you should write by standard input. And what is written by standard netcat input is responsible for sending it to the other end of the communication. Voilà! A poor web server.

This example will have made it clear to you why IP addresses can only be set by the system administrator. Otherwise, it would be trivial to make man-in-the-middle attacks against the users of that computer. I think you can delete that address from the loopback interface.

```
pi @ raspberrypi: ~ $ sudo ip addr of 161.67.137.169 dev lo
Raspberry Pi pi @: ~ $ ▄
```

You already know how to communicate data, but not only between two terminals of the same computer. If you are connected to the network, try connecting the two netcat by running each one on a different computer. You already know how to communicate data with TCP / IP!

Chapter 8 - Transmission Control Protocol

Internet is much more hostile than you can see with a test on your own Raspberry Pi. Communications between computers that are more than ten thousand kilometers away involve dozens of intermediate devices. There is a negligible probability that something is not going well. Message losses or even network reorganizations are normal during the same communication process. What should you do then? The answer is both simple and comforting: nothing. What can be done is already done by the underlying protocol, TCP (Transmission Control Protocol). When you used netcat, you were using TCP without knowing it. It is a transport protocol built on IP. This protocol provides mechanisms for flow control, fragmentation, reassembly, data integrity, reordering, and retransmission so that the communication experience is as close as possible to the ideal, even if things are not going well. It is so important that the entire family of Internet protocols is called TCP / IP, although TCP and IP are only two protocols in the family.

There is no doubt that he has succeeded. The vast majority of large-scale Internet services are built on TCP: the web, email, instant messaging systems, the directory service, and virtually everything that requires end-to-end encryption.

However, to provide TCP delivery guarantees, you have to use a series of time-consuming mechanisms, and it is a time that is not easily controllable. It is said that TCP introduces unbounded latency. That is, it is not possible to quantify exactly the maximum time it will take for a message to reach its destination, or even set an upper limit.

Think of systems that require a response in a limited time. It is what is known as real time systems. There are all kinds, from machinery control systems to multimedia systems.

Critical Real Time Systems (Hard Real-Time Systems). A control system of a robot, an airplane, or a helicopter cannot raise the indefinite retransmission of messages. If there is a problem, it must be treated in time to guarantee the safety of the users and the physical integrity of the device at all times. Sometimes the response times cannot exceed a handful of microseconds, and if it does not respond in time, the result can be fatal. These types of systems cannot be treated with GNU / Linux, as we have seen so far. We do not rule out a future book for this type of system, but it certainly goes beyond the objectives of the current course.

Soft Real-Time Systems. In other cases, the answer in a limited time is desirable but has no catastrophic consequences if it is not met. It is the case of multimedia systems. When voice and video communications are made, it is desirable that the arrival rate be more or less constant and, above all, that delays of more than the duration of the buffer do not accumulate. If it is not fulfilled, we will see cuts in the video and annoying metallic clicks in the audio. These types of systems can be treated without problems with GNU / Linux, but TCP is usually not the best possible option.

Unreliable Datagram Protocol

All real-time systems have a common requirement: they need to reduce latency to the minimum possible. Latency is the time that passes from when a message is sent until it is delivered at the other end.

To address these problems, there is a complementary protocol of TCP, the Unreliable Datagram Protocol (UDP). In UDP, there is no flow control; there are no retransmissions; there is no reordering; there is nothing more than routing and guarantee of integrity. I mean, we know how to take the messages to their destination, and if they arrive, they are sure to be sent. That's it. They can arrive in a different order from the delivery, and they can get lost along the way, they can even be duplicated. And the emissary will never have any feedback on whether the message has been received correctly or not. Little, right?

The positive part is that the latency, especially in networks with losses or congested, is significantly lower. So, it is used for video and audio broadcast. Because of its simplicity, it is also often used to communicate with very small devices (8-bit microcontrollers, FPGAs, etc.). All necessary guarantees remain the responsibility of the application. For example, if you need confirmations, you must send UDP messages requesting those confirmations.

Well, enough theory, get to work. Prepare the two terminals as in the case of the previous TCP communication and execute the following in the first.

pi @ raspberrypi: ~ $ nc -u -l 8888

This is the UDP server. Server is the name of the passive role in communication, the one that waits. That doesn't mean he doesn't talk, but he doesn't speak until someone (a client) starts a conversation. On the other terminal run the client:

pi @ raspberrypi: ~ $ nc -u 127.0.0.1 8888

Try to transfer data in both directions. As you can see, it works in a very similar way, and you will not be able to appreciate the difference if you do not use relatively distant equipment and somewhat congested networks. For the purposes of the book, they are practically equivalent, and we will opt for one or the other according to the requirements of the application.

Wireshark

When network communications are used, problems of all kinds appear very frequently. How do we diagnose them? The easiest way is to use a traffic capture and analysis tool. On your Raspberry Pi, you already have one of the best tools available: Wireshark.

Wireshark Initial Screen

When starting, the application shows something similar to the figure. A list appears with the network interfaces that we already know and some more that escapes what is intended with this book. Select the loopback interface: lo and press Start.

Now repeat the example of TCP and UDP communication we have done in this chapter. It is interesting even to make a mistake on purpose. Try, for example, to run the UDP client without a server at the other end.

Message Capture from the * Loopback * Interface

The normal thing in a network is to see hundreds of packages, and it is relatively difficult to find what we want to examine. That's why Wireshark incorporates very advanced filtering features. For the capture by clicking on the red square button, and we will filter the packages that interest us. For example, we will see the TCP packets destined for the port you have used. To do this, click Expression... You will have a dialog like the one in the figure in which you can write TCP to find all the TCP fields.

Capture Filter Editing

Display all the TCP protocol parameters and select tcp.port. In the Relation column, choose ==, and in the Value column, choose the port number you used. To finish press OK. Now, you will see in the Filter box the expression you have selected, some of the style at tcp.port == 3040. But we have not yet applied it. Press the button Apply. Only the conversation that interests us appears. As you can see, things are more complicated than they seem:

TCP conversation with a single message (Len other than 0).

The first three messages are the connection establishment (triple handshake), and until the fourth message, we do not see what we have sent. In the center window, the different elements of each captured message are dissected.

Another very useful option is full flow tracking. Right-click on any of the messages at the top of the screen and select the Follow TCP Stream option in the context menu that appears.

TCP Flow Tracking

The entire data exchange sequence appears without all the TCP paraphernalia. Only the data. In blue in one direction and in red in the other. In addition, we can select only the traffic in one of the directions. This is extraordinarily useful when we want to replicate the behavior of other programs.

Networking

The history of communication networks between computers is closely related to the history of Unix and, therefore, indirectly with GNU / Linux. At the University of California, Berkeley, the original idea of Unix, in which everything is an archive, was generalized to the networks. Communications are scheduled very similar to the use of files. These special files are called sockets.

The socket- based programming interface (API socket) remains the dominant one today to deal with communications networks and is the one we will see in the corresponding chapter.

In any case, it is convenient to give some small notions of the general fundamentals before writing code. In the introduction to GNU, in chapter 1 of this book, we already talk about file descriptors. These are numbers that represent the files from the point of view of the operating system. They basically provide an interface based on four basic operations, which correspond to system calls (operating system services):

The open call opens a file. Search for the file in the file system using a hierarchical name called the file path and assign a new file descriptor. From this moment, we can forget the route. The operating system only needs the descriptor. The close call closes the file. With this, the operating system terminates all ongoing operations that affect the file and releases its descriptor so that it can be reused with another file. The write call writes a set of octets to the file, and the read call reads a set of octets from the file.

This programming interface is used in GNU for a multitude of operations, operations with files on the disk, writing messages on the terminal, reading data from the keyboard, reading mouse events, etc. It seems logical that it also extends to network communications programming, and that is what the socket interface does.

A network connection does not have any element on the disk that represents it. Therefore, there is no choice but to replace the open call with another equivalent that provides the information necessary for communication. That call is called socket and is what gives name to the programming interface. The so-called socket assigns a file descriptor to a communication channel. But the communication channel is not enough, and we need to provide the data about the recipient or the origin of each message (IP addresses used, TCP or UDP ports, etc.). This is done with a new connect call for the client side or bind for the server side. When the socket is connected, it already works as a normal file descriptor.

From that moment on, all file descriptor calls are also valid (read, write, and close are also operations that can be performed on sockets once they are connected).

UDP communications do not need more calls, that's all. It is so similar that in some operating systems such as Plan9 or 2k, sockets are created with open calls using a special file path. However, GNU provides other sendto or recvfrom calls that only combine the write call with the connect call and the read call with the bind call. We will not use them at all.

However, TCP is more complex. To provide additional guarantees, the concept of connection needs to be implemented, such as the establishment of a new single channel between the two communicating processes. On the client side, it's simple; just connect do this job. The connection, in this case, is not simply to assign the destination address but to reserve a series of resources for communication with the destination.

The TCP server side is the most complex. Each client that connects to the server must have its own connection. With socket and bind, we can create a socket that serves messages destined for a specific address and a specific port, but only one. The solution goes through one more call, accept, which creates another new socket on each connection from a client process. The API is completed with a listen call that must be invoked to configure how many almost simultaneous connections it is possible to handle.

Although there are many more details that we have not mentioned, I think it can be used to understand how communications are programmed. These tables can be used to understand the sequence of operations that must be performed.

Chapter 9 - C Development

For the first time, the book will be held in a multi-language version (C and Python). We hope in this way to accommodate a greater number of students. Currently, we use Python as the first language of the degree (first semester of the first year, Computer Science subject), but until this course, we have used C. Therefore, there is a group of students who feel more comfortable with C and another that feels more comfortable with Python.

This book tries to divide the content so that you don't have to read everything if you are interested in only one of these languages. In this chapter, we will describe the set of tools that we will use to make C programs and a simple example of their use.

The First Program

It is tradition to start with a first program that simply writes the message Hello, World on the screen. It goes back to the origins of BCPL, the precursor of C.

Start an order terminal and create a folder to enter the examples in this chapter. We will work in that folder. For example:

pi @ raspberrypi: ~ $ mkdir test
pi @ raspberrypi: ~ $ cd test
Raspberry Pi pi @: ~ / test $ ▄

Use a text editor to write the following program in a file named hello.c. As a text editor
you can use Leafpad, simply by clicking on the icon or from the command line with Leafpad hello.c.

```
#include <stdio.h>
int main () {
puts ("Hello, World");
return 0;
}
```

Save the file to the folder you created and return to the terminal:

pi @ raspberrypi: ~ / test $ make hello
cc hello.c -o hello Raspberry Pi pi @: ~ / test $ ▃

The C program has been compiled by GNU make (make), which in turn has run the C (cc) compiler to generate the hello executable. Note that GNU executables do not have a distinctive extension.

Now we can execute it:

pi @ raspberrypi: ~ / test $./hello
Hello World
Raspberry Pi pi @: ~ / test $ ▃

Notice that we have written a period and a bar in front to indicate where the file is located. It is a relative route, of which we have already spoken.

You will wonder why we have to indicate the path for this executable and not for Leafpad, for example. The operational system finds the executables either because the user explicitly tells them where they are or because they are in a series of folders that are known as system paths. Obviously, the current folder is not in the system paths, because you just created it, so our only option is to indicate the path.
Warning You may read texts that recommend you add the folder. (the work folder) to the system paths. Do not do it, it is a bad idea in general, but especially for security reasons.

The C Compiler

In GNU / Linux, there are several C compilers. The most used is that of the GNU (GNU Compiler Collection) project that is invoked with the gcc or simply cc command. Normally we will not compile the C files by hand, but we will do it through a construction tool, specifically GNU make.

The C compiler can be used as a compiler, as an editor or as both. For example, back to our program hello.c and type in the terminal the following:

pi @ raspberrypi: ~ / test $ gcc -c hello.c
pi @ raspberrypi: ~ / test $ ls
hello hello.c hello.o
Raspberry Pi pi @: ~ / test $ ▄

Now we have a hello.o file. It is an object file with the machine instructions corresponding to the hello.c file but without the structure of an executable. Multiple object files can be combined to generate a single executable using the editor. In GNU you can use the C compiler itself to mount the executable:

pi @ raspberrypi: ~ / test $ gcc -o hello hello.o
Raspberry Pi pi @: ~ / test $ ▄
When we do not use the -c option, the compiler behaves as an editor and, if necessary, as a compiler simultaneously. If we do not specify an executable name with the -o option, the compiler will generate one with a.out name. This is so for historical reasons, so it is clear that we usually must specify the -o option.

Multiple Source Files

An executable can be composed from several source files. For example, divide the program into a hello.c file which has the main program and uses a function that is defined in another file named fc:

```
#include <stdio.h>
void say_hello () {
puts ("Hello, World");
}
```

Now the hello.c file would be something like this:

```
void say_hello (void);
int main () {
say hi();
return 0;
}
```

To generate the executable, you would have to compile both files and then mount them:

```
pi @ raspberrypi: ~ / test $ gcc -c hello.c fc
pi @ raspberrypi: ~ / test $ gcc -o hello hello.o fo
Raspberry Pi pi @: ~ / test $ ▄
```

We are going to change the program so that it greets and says goodbye. In addition to the function say_hello (now in the file f_hola.c) we will have another function say_adios (in the file f_adios.c).

```
pi @ raspberrypi: ~ / test $ mv fc f_hola.c
pi @ raspberrypi: ~ / test $ cp f_hola.c f_adios.c
pi @ raspberrypi: ~ / test $ leafpad f_adios.c
```

Now change the f_adios.c file to say goodbye:

```
#include <stdio.h>
say goodbye () {
puts ("Goodbye, World");
}
```

And the main program hello.c to call the two functions:

```
void say_hello (void);
void say_bye (void);
int main () {
say hi();
say goodbye();
return 0;
}
```

This is more like a real show. The main program calls several functions that are spread over other files. But it is not usual to put the declaration of functions directly in the main file. It is better to put those statements in a header file that is included when needed.

For example, edit a new file greet.h   with the declarations of the two functions:

```
#ifndef SALUDAR_H
#define SALUDAR_H
void say_hello (void);
void say_bye (void);
#endif
And use it in hello.c:
#include "greet.h"
int main () {
say hi();
say goodbye();
return 0;
}
```

Now we can compile everything:

```
Raspberry Pi pi @: ~ / test $ gcc -c hello.c f_hola.c f_adios.c
Raspberry Pi pi @: ~ / test $ gcc -o hello f_hola.o hello.o
f_adios.o
```

Raspberry Pi pi @: ~ / test $ ▁

Note that the header file does not need to be compiled because it has nothing but declarations and is included where necessary.

Program Libraries

When programs grow, a more flexible organization mechanism becomes necessary. For example, we can group several of the object files in a library and then mount the executable with the library. For example, we are going to put the files f_hola.o and f_adios.o in a libsaludar.a library, and then we build the executable with this library. To create the library, we will use the program ar (archiver):

pi @ raspberrypi: ~ / test $ ar rcs libsaludar.a f_hola.o f_adios.o pi @ raspberrypi: ~ / test $ gcc -L. -o hello hello.o -lsaludar Raspberry Pi pi @: ~ / test $ ▁

The ar program is somewhat similar to the archives that are used to create compressed files (WinZip, WinRAR, 7zip, PeaZip, etc.) unless, in this case, it is not compressed. In GNU, compression and archiving are separate processes, so that the user can choose how to archive and how to compress independently.

In the same libsaludar.a file, we can put any number of object files with any number of functions. However, when building the executable with gcc, things do not change even if the number of files and functions grows.

Libraries are usually made in a separate folder. For example:

pi @ raspberrypi: ~ / test $ mkdir greeting
pi @ raspberrypi: ~ / test $ mv *.h f_ * greeting

pi @ raspberrypi: ~ / test $ cd greeting
pi @ raspberrypi: ~ / test / greeting $ gcc -c *.c
pi @ raspberrypi: ~ / test / greeting $ ar rcs libsaludar.a *.o
pi @ raspberrypi: ~ / test / greeting $ cd..
Raspberry Pi pi @: ~ / test $ ▄

Now the library is in the greeting subfolder and the main program in the parent folder. To compile hello.c we have to tell the compiler where the header files can be and when mounting hello, we must indicate the new folder where to look for libraries:

Raspberry Pi pi @: ~ / test $ gcc -c hello.c -Isaludo
Raspberry Pi pi @: ~ / test $ gcc -o hello -Lsaludo hello.o -lsaludar
Raspberry Pi pi @: ~ / test $

The GNU Make Construction Tool

As we have seen, as soon as the program starts to grow a little, the process of building the executable can be really tedious. The make program that we already used in the first example allows us to automate the construction.

$ (CC) $ (CFLAGS) -c $ <

Anatomy of a Make Recipe.

C Development

Except in the trivial cases, you need a configuration file that tells you how to build the executable. It must be called makefile, Makefile, or GNUmakefile. It basically consists of recipes in which you explain how to build a file from a specified set of files. So, in our last example we can make a makefile inside the greeting subfolder like this one:

libsaludar.a: f_hola.o f_adios.o
ar rcs $ @ $ ^

This rule reads like this: to build libsaludar.a, you must first build f_hola.o and f_adios.o and then execute ar rcs libsaludar.o f_hola.o f_adios.o. Notice that we use the abbreviation $ @ to represent the purpose of the rule (libsaludar.a) and $ ^ to represent the dependencies of the rule (everything that follows the colon). And how do we tell you how to make the object files f_hola.o and f_adios.o ? It is not necessary. GNU make knows how to make them from C files with the same name. Internally you have already defined a recipe like this:

%.o:%.c
$ (CC) $ (CFLAGS) -c $ <

That reads to build an object file from a C file of the same name you must execute where the symbol $ < corresponds to a special GNU make variable.

The recipes already included in GNU make it virtually unnecessary to define new rules except in very simple cases. The interesting thing about this is that the make rules use a wide variety of variables that already have a default value, but that we can change to adjust the operation.

Now just run make clean to delete the generated files and leave only the code we have written.

An interesting aspect of the use of make is that it only generates what is necessary, and the rules affected by files that have changed apply. That is, if a good makefile is available, just run make so that everything you need is compiled and only what is necessary at any time.

If the makefile does not have all the dependencies, GNU make will not know if it has to rebuild any file. For example, in this small example, we have not added hello.o dependencies with greeting / greeting.h. The correct thing would have been to add a rule in which only the dependency is indicated:

hello.o: hello.c greeting / greeting.h

If you do not want to complicate makefile just keep it in mind, and when you modify something that is not in the dependencies, we can force the compilation with:

pi @ raspberrypi: ~ / test $ make -C greeting -B
pi @ raspberrypi: ~ / test $ make -B

The first order forces the construction of the library, and the second forces the construction of the executable.

Debugging Programs with GNU Debugger

The construction of correct programs requires the close cooperation of two very simple but very important techniques: testing and debugging.

The test consists in the elaboration of small programs that show that our functions do what they are supposed to do. There is nothing to replace this, and it is essential in any software development process. We will discuss this topic later.

The other technique that complements the test is debugging, which consists in the elimination of errors (bugs) previously detected in the tests. Debugging is a relatively simple process in the form and totally systematic, but surprisingly difficult in practice.

No special tool is needed to debug. A set of carefully chosen printf statements or any other way to examine the contents of the memory can be used. GNU debugger (abbreviated gdb) is therefore not strictly necessary, but it can save you a huge amount of time.

Debugging tools allow you to stop the execution of the program at specific points, for example, just before the occurrence of an error in which it is known that the execution ends unexpectedly. Stopping the program allows you to explore the memory at that point, including knowing the value of the processor's variables and records and moving forward through the execution until you find the exact point at which the program dysfunction occurs.

The Debugging Process

Let's talk a little first about the process of eliminating errors. It is important because experience tells us that it is counter-intuitive, and we naturally tend to skip essential steps.

Program errors can be classified in several ways. It is very common to classify them according to their visibility and persistence:

	Visible	Hidden
Persistent	Ideal	Unknown
Transient	Hard	Very difficult

A visible error is one that has been detected because the program does not do what it should. On the contrary, a hidden error is one that has not been detected, although it exists, either because the code it affects is executed very rarely or because there is another error that masks it. Visible errors are usually detected in tests and do not usually reach the code in production. However, the hidden ones reach the production code and can have disastrous consequences. Ariane 5 or Therac 25 are some examples that we should all remember. Search Google if you don't know them.

On the other hand, they can also be classified as persistent errors when errors manifest themselves in all programs or transient executions when they only manifest in some executions or at unpredictable moments.

Obviously, the ideals for their elimination are visible and persistent errors, and we have to do everything possible so that the possible errors are of this type. For that, defensive programming techniques and memory debugging tools such as Valgrind are used. It is outside the scope of this course to talk about the latter, but we recommend that you try them if you encounter an elusive error.

Usually, the errors are detected in the tests, and even if this is not the case, we should make a small test program that reproduces the error. Therefore, we can assume that there is a relatively short program that does not do what we expect. The key is to apply debugging consistent with the following process:

- Study the data. See which tests fail and which ones succeed.
- Develop a hypothesis consistent with the data.
- Design an experiment to refute the hypothesis. Decide how to interpret the result of the experiment a priori, before performing it.
- Keep a record of everything.

The design stage of the experiment is also very systematic. The aim is to narrow the search space, either by reducing the range of data to be analyzed or by limiting the region of the program where the error is located.

Typically, a small program is designed that exercises the functions that may contain the error. From this failed test case, a binary search of the error is performed. If the program does not work correctly, it is because some of the values returned or stored are not what we expected. Approximately at the midpoint, we will have to check if the intermediate values calculated so far are as expected. If they are correct, the error must be in the second half; otherwise, it would be in the first half. We repeat this process until we find the point of error.

It is at this stage of the debugging process that debuggers such as GNU debugger can be useful. Of course, we can always examine the intermediate values with a printf in the right place. But every time, we have to examine another point we will have to recompile the program. The debugger, on the other hand, allows you to examine and modify any program data and stop the execution of the program at any point.

Using GNU Debugger

In order for gdb to be fully exploited, it is necessary to compile the program with support for debugging. This is specified with the compiler -ggdb option. Typically, it is done by adding this option to the CFLAGS variable of the makefile.

Using the command-line interface, the first step is to invoke gdb specifying the executable to debug:

pi @ raspberrypi: ~ / test $ gdb hello
GNU gdb (Raspbian 7.7.1 + dfsg-5) 7.7.1
...
Reading symbols from hello... done.
(gdb) ▁

Displays the GDB prompt indicating that you wait for an order.

Watchpoints

A watchpoint is an indication to the debugger to interrupt the execution of the program each time the value of a variable is read or modified. Several GDB orders allow us to work with them.

Alter Variables and Flow

It is common for more than one error to be detected in a GDB session. Sometimes it may be interesting to temporarily fix a problem to find another without recompiling. With GDB, it is possible to set values to variables or alter the normal sequence of execution.

Work with Processes

Some of our programs will be multithreaded. GDB allows working with multiple processes simultaneously, even if they correspond to different executables.

Work with Threads

We will also sometimes use the threads. It is a much more efficient concurrency mechanism than processes, but significantly more prone to hard-to-find errors.

Chapter 10 - Programming the Peripherals

We will now see a series of C programming examples of the elements we have seen in Chapter 2. Our goal is to provide an overview of the full range of possibilities we have available using C language. That implies that we are not going to limit to using a library, but all that I know at the moment.

When you face a new project, you have to understand all the elements involved. This usually involves exploring, testing, and reading. Your first objective has to be to reduce uncertainty, to have enough details to avoid having to look at the datasheet of the devices at every step when we are designing the application.

Do not take these examples as a sample of how to program, and we will see that later. It's about learning to use peripherals from your favorite programming language. Therefore, we try to make the code as simple and straightforward as possible, not the most maintainable, not even the most readable. We give priority to the use of the API offered by each library.

Digital Inputs and Outputs in C

For the programming of digital inputs and outputs in C, we have three libraries available: wiringPi by Gordon Henderson, bcm2835 by Mike McCauley, and pigpio by joan@abyz.co.uk. All of them are more or less equivalent for the purposes of the book, although each has its advantages and disadvantages. To start, I recommend you use WiringPi. Let's look at examples with all three.

Digital Inputs and Outputs with WiringPi

Check out the WiringPi reference book and especially the main functions. If you try to execute it, you will probably get a message that indicates that user pi does not have enough privileges. In that case, you have to run it with sudo. This is going to be quite frequent in software that manipulates physical devices.
No serious operating system can allow a normal user to directly manipulate the devices. It could even compromise the physical integrity of the system.

We can also program the generation of PWM signals with the help of the WiringPi library. The base frequency for PWM in Raspberry Pi is 19.2Mhz. This frequency can be divided by using a divisor indicated with pwmSetClock, up to a maximum of 4095. At this frequency the internal algorithm that generates the sequence of pulses, but in the case of the BCM2835 are two operating modes, a mode balanced (balanced) which is difficult to control the pulse width, but allows a PWM control very high frequency, and a mode mark and space which is much more intuitive and more appropriate to control servos. The balanced mode is appropriate for controlling the power supplied to the load or for transmitting information.

In the mark and space mode, the PWM module will increase an internal counter until it reaches a configurable limit, the PWM range, which can be a maximum of 1024. At the beginning of the cycle, the pin will be set to 1 logical and will remain until the internal counter reaches the value set by the user. At that time, the pin will be set to 0 logical and will remain until the end of the cycle.

Let's see its application to the control of a servomotor. A

servomotor has a signal input to indicate the desired inclination. Every 20ms expect a pulse, and the width of this pulse determines the inclination of the servo. Around 1.5ms is the pulse width necessary for the centered position. A smaller width rotates the servo counterclockwise (up to approximately 1ms), and a longer duration makes it rotate clockwise (up to approximately 2ms). In this case, the range and the divisor must be calculated so that the pulse is produced every 20ms, and the control of the pulse width around 1.5ms is with the maximum possible resolution.

The assembly is as following. The red servo cable (V +) is connected to + 5V in P1-2 or P1-4, the black or brown cable (V-) to GND in P1-6, and the yellow, orange, or white (signal) cable to GPIO18 on P1-12. No other components are needed.

```
#include <wiringPi.h>
#include <stdlib.h>
int main (int argc, char * argv [])
{
if (argc <5) {
printf ("Usage:% s divisor range min max \ n", argv [0]);
exit (0);
}
int div = atoi (argv [1]);
int range = atoi (argv [2]);
int min = atoi (argv [3]);
int max = atoi (argv [4]);
wiringPiSetupGpio ();
pinMode (18, PWM_OUTPUT);
pwmSetMode (PWM_MODE_MS);
pwmSetClock (div);
pwmSetRange (range);
for (;;) {
pwmWrite (18, min);
delay (1000);
pwmWrite (18, max);
delay (1000);
```

}
}

To have maximum control of the servo position, we will test with the maximum range of 1024. In that case, the divisor must be such that the frequency of the PWM pulse is:

$$f = \frac{\text{base f}}{\text{range} \times \text{div}} = \frac{19.2 \times 10^6 \text{ Hz}}{1024 \times \text{div}} = \frac{1}{20 \text{ ms}} = 50 \text{ Hz}$$

That is, the splitter should be set to 390. The full range of the servo depends on the specific model. Theoretically, it should be between 52 and 102, the value being fully centered 77. In practice, the specific servo will have to be tested. Our experiments give a useful range between 29 and 123 for the TowerPro microservo available in the laboratory.

Programming Digital Inputs and Outputs with BCM2835

The bcm2835 library is a very fine wrapper of hardware capabilities. That is, it practically describes in C what appears on the Broadcom datasheet. In this sense, it is ideal to explore the architecture and extract the maximum juice from your Raspberry Pi. For non-trivial tasks, you will have no choice but to study well to understand how it works.

As for the handling of digital inputs and outputs, the bcm2835 library has an interface very similar to WiringPi but supports many more capabilities of the underlying hardware. In this book, we will not use the advanced features.

An interesting feature of the programs that use bcm2835 is that they do not need to be executed as superuser if they only access the GPIO pins, it is enough that the user belongs to the gpio group.

```
#include <bcm2835.h>
int main () {
bcm2835_init ();
bcm2835_gpio_fsel (18, BCM2835_GPIO_FSEL_OUTP);
for (int v = 0;; v =! v) {
bcm2835_gpio_write (18, v);
bcm2835_delay (1000);
}
bcm2835_close ();
}
```

As you can see, the code is practically equivalent to wiringPi. The compilation is also similar. To compile it, we can make a makefile file almost equivalent to the wiringPi example.

```
CFLAGS = -I / usr / local / include
LDFLAGS = -L / usr / local / lib
LDLIBS = -lbcm2835
test-gpio: test-gpio.o
```

Regardless of the name of the library, we see that it is necessary to indicate that you look for header files in / usr / local / include and look for the libraries in / usr / local / lib. This is because bcm2835 is not yet as a system package, and we have installed it manually.

Among the advanced features bcm2835 implements the possibility of changing the value of a set of hit pins, of reading a set of hit pins, better control over the events of rising, falling, or leveling flank events, etc.

PWM with BCM2835

When programming, the pulse width modulation bcm2835 requires a little knowledge of the hardware operation. For example, it requires knowing that the two PWM channels are not associated with a single pin and that one or the other channel can be associated with some of the pins by selecting specific alternative functions. Following the same example of wiringPi, we will configure the GPIO18 pin as PWM output. For this, we will have to select the alternative function 5 of that pin, which corresponds to the PWM0 channel. Do you understand now the utility of the flyer that we give you in the book? From that moment, we only work with the channel, not with the pin.

```
#include <bcm2835.h>
#include <stdio.h>
int main (int argc, char * argv [])
{
if (argc <5) {
printf ("Usage:% s divisor range min max \ n", argv [0]);
exit (0);
}
int div = atoi (argv [1]);
int range = atoi (argv [2]);
int min = atoi (argv [3]);
int max = atoi (argv [4]);
bcm2835_init ();
bcm2835_gpio_fsel (18, BCM2835_GPIO_FSEL_ALT5);
bcm2835_pwm_set_clock (div);
bcm2835_pwm_set_mode (0, 1, 1);
bcm2835_pwm_set_range (0, range);
for (;;) {
bcm2835_pwm_set_data (0, min);
bcm2835_delay (1000);
bcm2835_pwm_set_data (0, max);
bcm2835_delay (1000);
}
bcm2835_close ();
return 0;
}
```

Programming Digital Inputs and Outputs with Pigpio

The pigpio library is halfway between the previous two. On the one hand, it implements a low-level interface that practically reproduces the Broadcom data-sheet in C. On the other hand. It implements abstraction layers that extend the functionality considerably. For example, it adds the possibility to simulate PWM modulation on any pin and incorporates very interesting debugging capabilities.

From the point of view of programming digital inputs and outputs, it is very similar to the other libraries.

```
#include <pigpio.h>
int main () {
gpioInitialise ();
gpioSetMode (18, PI_OUTPUT);
for (int v = 0;; v =! v) {
gpioWrite (18, v);
gpioDelay (1000000);
}
gpioTerminate ();
}
```

Virtually identical to the other examples except for the names of the functions. The compilation is very similar to the examples in bcm2835 because the pigpio library is also not available as a system package, and we have had to install it manually.

```
CFLAGS = -I / usr / local / include -pthread
LDFLAGS = -L / usr / local / lib -pthread
LDLIBS = -lpigpio -lpthread
test-gpio: test-gpio.o
```

An important difference with respect to the other libraries is that you have to enable the use of threads and add the system's thread library. This is necessary because many of the added capabilities of pigpio are implemented as threads.

PWM Modulation with Pigpio

PWM modulation with pigpio can be done with low-level functions equivalent to what is done in bcm2835 but also supports a much simpler high-level interface. There is a function to control servos with PWM and another to control the duty-cycle, and with it, the power delivered to a load.

It is not necessary to specify low-level parameters, just the pulse width in milliseconds. A width of zero for the PWM signal. The remaining valid values are between 500 and 2500, although the actual servo range depends on the specific model.

Another interesting feature of pigpio is that these functions can be applied to any pin. If it is one of those that supports PWM by hardware, it will use it transparently and, if not, simulate it with a separate thread. The frequency of the PWM signal it generates is, in all cases, 50Hz.

Exercises

Do not try to use all libraries at once. Choose one and wait to feel comfortable with it to try another. At the moment, we propose the following exercises.
1.   Configure and program the hardware and software necessary to have two LEDs flashing at the same rate but keeping only one of them on at the same time.
2.   Modify the previous example so that switching takes place only when a button is pressed. One of the LEDs will be on when the button is not pressed, and the other will be on

only when the button is pressed.

Challenges for the Week

1.	Moderate: Design a mechanism to control an array of LEDs of at least 16x32 with the Raspberry Pi.

Chapter 11 - I2C Interface Programming

The precise programming of an I2C device depends a lot on the manufacturer. In general, we will first need a configuration, and then we will enter a loop that reads or writes data. For example, let's see how the MPU6050 accelerometer is handled.

I2C programming with wiringPi

As always, wiringPi sacrifices flexibility for the sake of greater simplicity. It does not even provide a function to change the clock frequency and does not support block transfers, but only 8 and 16-bit registers.

I2C Programming with BCM2835

In bcm2835, the interface is also simple, but a file descriptor is not required for each I2C device, and the communication is a bit cumbersome because the addressing of the records must be done manually with a write.

Actually, the library supports some other functions to deal with special cases. If you face a new I2C module, consult the documentation of bcm2835 in case it makes things easier for you.

I2C Programming with Pigpio

The pigpio library implements an interface that combines the two previous approaches. You can read or write bytes or words, but also blocks, which significantly simplifies the program. It also allows access to the two I2C buses.

As in the rest of the pigpio modules, it is the most complete of the three, and bcm2835 is the closest to the hardware and, therefore, the smallest. Our personal recommendation is that you use wiringPi to start, for its simplicity.

Chapter 12 – SPI C Programming

The three libraries we have used for programming digital inputs and outputs also support the use of the SPI interface. SPI modules benefit from concurrent sending and receiving capacity, and very reasonable rates (30MHz) can be achieved

SPI Programming with WiringPi

Programming is simple in that it only uses two functions, but it can be really complicated to understand communication with some SPI devices. The reason is that in SPI to be able to read data, and you have to write data; in fact, it is read at the same time it is written. This means that in real devices, you have to make many transactions that are completely discarded.

The wiringPiSPISetup function initializes the communication for channel 0 to 10Mz. There are two channels available (0 and 1) that use the same legs except for the selection SPI_CE0 and SPI_CE1, respectively.

Calls to wiringPiSPIDataRW to perform an SPI transaction where a concurrent set of bytes is written and read. The precise meaning of what is read and written depends on the device and in some cases may require discarding part or all of the information. In this case, the first byte is the order, and then the arguments are sent.

Simplicity is maximum, but hardware capabilities are also lost to accommodate all SPI transfer modes. More details can be found in the Gordon Henderson article available at projects.drogon.net.

The problem with wiringPi is that for SPI transfers, it is not possible to select the mode. The author considers that the vast majority of SPI modules use mode 0. It may be true, but the

ADS1118 we use in the book is mode 1.
Warning The wiringPi library assumes that we use SPI0 with mode 0. For this reason, we do not recommend it because the CJMCU-1118 module uses mode 1.

SPI Programming with BCM2835

In the bcm2835 library, we have a range of functions closer to hardware. Some functions are similar to wiringPi, but it adds many more to configure the transfer mode and the SPI interface.

Although it seems more complex, it is really due to the greater control of initialization. Initialization is longer, but the possibility of using different transmission and reception buffers simplifies many frequent cases.

SPI Programming with Pigpio

With pigpio, it is possible to use the auxiliary peripheral SPI (SPI1) in addition to the main one (see flag A of the flag field in spiOpen). The advantage is that this other SPI interface has configurable word size and three available chip lines (instead of two). On the other hand, the main interface is noticeably faster, so we will use that normally.

Measure Times Accurately

The measurement of the discharge time of a capacitor has been proposed as a technique to measure analog quantities using the digital inputs of the Raspberry Pi. Adafruit's proposal uses the number of iterations of a loop to measure time. As they themselves recognize, this is not very accurate.

Raspbian is a timeshare system. The Raspberry Pi runs several programs at once, and this implies that the processor can evict our program to run another program. In that case, the number of iterations of the loop will be significantly less than normal. But how do we know if there has been eviction? The sad reality is that a user program cannot know it; it has no control over this. This is not even the only cause of uncertainty, and there may be interference from interrupt handlers, device handlers, etc.

But there is a way to measure time quite accurately, using the MISO leg of the SPI interface and a digital output leg.

Suppose we have a sensor device whose measurement materializes in the value of a resistor. It can be an LDR, as in the case of the Adafruit article, or a simple potentiometer, or a thermistor, or a piezoresistive sensor, or a magnetoresistive sensor,... We build an RC circuit similar to the figure.

We discharge the condenser by putting the GPIO22 leg low for a sufficient time. We configure the GPIO22 leg as an input so that it is high impedance, and we start a large SPI transfer. The buffer must be full of zeros until the capacitor charge is sufficient to be interpreted as a 1. The first non-zero byte marks the instant in which the capacitor is reasonably charged. This time is proportional to RC, and, therefore, to R. A calibration can be performed to measure with absolute precision, but in any case, we have a precise measurement that allows us to compare.

The code is extremely simple. We provide it only in wiringPi.

Assembly for precise measurement of a resistor.
The program prints the buffer position where the input begins to be nonzero and the first nonzero value. That position would have to be multiplied by 8 to translate it into SCLK cycles and could be adjusted with the value to obtain the exact number of

cycles.

The accuracy depends on the clock period used. In the example, we have used a 500KHz clock, but it can be up to 32MHz safely. The problem is that the larger the clock, the greater the buffer we have to use in the SPI transfer.

For buffers larger than 4KB, you must specify it in the kernel command line (/boot/cmdline.txt) and restart the Raspberry Pi. For example, for 256KB, it would be added:

spidev.bufsiz = 262144

The code can be improved by a bisection search. It is deliberately simple to be understood from the conceptual point of view. The result is that we could measure RC with an accuracy of up to 1/32 us. If we use a 1uF capacitor, this implies that we can measure R with an accuracy of 1/32 Ohm. Even if we use the 500KHz clock, we will have an accuracy of 2 Ohm, which is also not bad.

Actual results may be somewhat worse due to jitter or instability in SCLK or resistance noise. A ceramic capacitor in parallel with the electrolytic can help remove high frequency noise. In any case, the method is much more precise than Adafruit's original proposal, and does not depend on the state of loading of the system.

Challenges for the Week

1. Easy Design a mechanism to control LED strips using the SPI interface.

Chapter 13 - udp_server_socket: Network Communications

Both B +, 2B, and 3B models include an Ethernet interface. The Raspberry Pi 4 B that we use in this book includes WiFi, but any of the others can also have WiFi for a price of about € 4 using a USB WiFi interface. Therefore, any Raspberry Pi project must consider the possibility of communicating data through a TCP / IP network.

To program on a network in GNU / Linux, as in most modern operating systems, a programming interface called API socket is used. It is a set of functions designed to make network programming closely resemble input / output with files.

In chapter 2, we have already introduced the socket interface. In C, this interface is included in the libc system library that is automatically incorporated.

Conclusion

Thank you for making it through to the end of *Raspberry Pi 4 Ultimate Guide*, let's hope it was informative and able to provide you with all of the tools you need to achieve your goals whatever they may be.

The Raspberry Pi, a small single board computer, also called a nano-computer, has gathered a considerable community around it. The many features available have delighted the makers and electronics enthusiasts of all kinds. Each new version of this software is always eagerly awaited.

Released recently, the new Raspberry Pi 4 convinces with its ARM Cortex-A72 1.5 GHz. In this new model, it is also possible to add 1 GB, 2 GB or even 4 GB of RAM, greatly increasing its computing power.

Some important interface changes make the Raspberry Pi a must-have. In particular, it has a LAN Gigabit LAN with up to 1000 Mbit and Bluetooth 5.0. Highly anticipated innovations in USB interfaces have emerged: in addition to the usual two USB 2.0 ports, the Raspberry Pi contains two USB 3.0 ports, as well as two micro HDMI interfaces compatible with 4K.

This book was an attempt to guide you to understand Raspberry Pi 4 a lot better and enjoy programming with it.

Finally, if you found this book useful in any way, a review on Amazon is always appreciated!

Description

This practical guide of the Raspberry-Pi 4 is a document that aims to help you get to know and master your Raspberry-Pi 4 a lot better. To do this, the guide steers you step by step to begin and then implement as easily as possible many practical and inexpensive achievements!

You can set up:
- A media center,
- A HiFi system,
- A download server,
- A personal cloud solution,
- An "Old School" console emulator,
- Using the GPIO (New) pins,
- A network supervisor,
- And a lot more...

You will also find all the necessary command lines and tips and tricks to master your small machine.

So, add this book to your cart today and enter the amazing world of Raspberry-Pi 4!!!

Raspberry Pi: Project Ideas Book

Discover a New World of Possibilities to Build and Develop Original Projects & Programs (Step-By-Step Updated Guide)

By

Ethan J. Upton

Table of Contents

Introduction

Congratulations on purchasing *Raspberry Pi 4: Project Ideas Book,* and thank you for doing so.

There are plenty of books on this subject on the market, thanks again for choosing this one! Every effort was made to ensure it is full of as much useful information as possible; please enjoy!

Raspberry Pi is a very small (credit card-sized) microcomputer. A few years ago, some members of Cambridge University and some English computer scientists decided to team up to form a foundation called the Raspberry Pi Foundation with one goal: to increase the number of computers available to children. They knew, however, that it would be necessary to create low-cost, programmable equipment priced at $ 25, the equivalent of a textbook. The main objective of the development team was to stimulate the teaching of basic computer science in schools.

In 2012, the credit-card-sized microcomputer was launched at $ 25, which naturally piqued the interest of the hardware, programming, Linux and beyond community...

Raspberry Pi Anatomy

Currently, Raspberry Pi comes in two versions - model A and model B. Both are the same size. The difference is in model B, which has one more USB port, has an ethernet port, and 512MB of RAM, unlike model A which has only 256MB of RAM. The processor is a 700MHz ARM, equivalent to the processor used in many of the smartphones in the market. It does not include any internal memory. However, it has an SD card slot.

Chapter 1 - Testing the Raspberry Pi as a Virtual Machine

After downloading, unzip the file into its own directory and either start the corresponding RaspberryPi.vmx file (VMware) or the RaspberryPi. ova file (Oracle Virtualbox). In this case, the virtualization software is automatically started, which takes the selected image into operation.

Here, of course, the virtual Raspberry does not have a "real" hard disk, but a "virtual" hard disk on the computer - nothing more than a container file set up by Virtualbox or VMware, then as a "hard drive" for the virtual machine, in this one Case Raspberry, to serve.

After starting the virtualization environment, log in to the virtual Raspberry Pi for the first time. Usually, the corresponding user name is pi - the corresponding default password is raspberry (all lowercase).

Switching off the Raspberry Pi via the console is done simply via the command sudo init 0 or via the graphical user interface. In this book, unless explicitly stated, the VMware image will be used to implement the Raspberry Pi in the virtual machine.

Stay Current: Keep Raspberry Fresh Via Update

Basically, it would not matter which version the operating system of the Raspberry Pi has in the used image. Because, assuming a fast broadband Internet connection, the operating system is brought up to date in a few minutes via command line.

Update the operating system and the installed applications -
in theory: Who - like the author - has decided to use the
VMware image, will encounter the first hurdle after the first
start of the virtual machine: The network for the Raspberry Pi
is not available.

The reason: The required etho network interface was not
available on the Raspberry Pi. To correct this error, the
Raspberry Pi virtual must be touched up manually. Once
that's done, get the mentioned commands to bring the
Raspberry Pi up to date.

Network Coupling: VMware and Raspberry Pi

Basically, you have several options for bringing the virtual
host and the physical computer together in terms of network
or to include the virtual host in the domestic network. The
most widely used variant is Bridged Mode, in which the virtual
machine gets its own IP address from the DSL / WLAN router
in your home network.

The NAT (Network Address Translation) mode, in which the
virtual machine and the physical computer share the IP
address, so to speak, is technically possible, but the problem is
the other way round - that is, if you have a connection from
the outside or another computer in the home network with the
guest record, is first time troubleshooting announced to find
out why the connection does not work right away.

Therefore: Use the bridge port of the virtualization software -
whether you use the Oracle or VMware product.

Restore Network Connection

Delete the so-called Mac address cache. The network interface
is now available, which can be checked via the ifconfig

command in the console. Subsequently, the update of the system via sudo apt-get update nothing in the way.

Using Keyboard Settings

Anyone who has used one or the other Unix command in the console of the virtual Raspberry Pi, may have noticed in the specification of parameters or options, that what it says on the keys, and what arrives in the console, a Small is little different - that is, a wrong configured Tasta-Tureinstellung is active. Who would like to use the German keyboard setting including use of the umlauts in the console, which gives in the console first the command:

sudo dpkg-reconfigure console-setup to start the configuration of the console.

Surf More Comfortably And Retrofit Your Browser

Here you will find tens of configuration pages, all of which are converted to German / German. For reasons of space, we did not print all of these here.

If you are unsure about an option, just keep the default settings. The settings made become active immediately after completing the wizard.

Depending on the Raspberry Pi image used in the virtual machine, an Internet browser is also available. But even old acquaintances such as Mozilla Firefox and Google Chrome (Chromium) can be retrofitted in a few simple steps:

You start the Google Chrome port with this command:
sudo apt-get install chromium browser
To install Mozilla Firefox use the command
sudo apt-get install firefox
No matter which browser you want to use: Less is more, you

can best set up just one browser for space reasons.

After starting the link, the installed web browser appears on the smart Raspberry Pi interface in the virtual machine.
Working and trying out the Raspberry Pi in the virtual machine is, of course, only half as exciting compared to the »real« Raspberry Pi - the use of the credit card-sized board is only really interesting in practice. If you have already informed yourself in advance about the Raspberry Pi on the Internet, you have probably already read that there are different revisions here.

Development continues not only in IT in general but also in the Raspberry Pi project. Every few months there is a development on both the software and on the hardware side to report: While the first Raspberry Pi, Model A, with only one USB port and no network connection was delivered, was the successor, model B, already with equipped with two USB ports and one RJ45-10 / 100-Mbit network interface.

In autumn 2012, the model B was replaced by a second B model (revision v2), which is equipped with more memory compared to its predecessor. While the first models are equipped with 256 MB of capacity, the B2 model now offers 512 MB - twice as much RAM.

Necessary Accessories For Raspberry Operation

In the time you wait for the delivery of your Raspberry Pi, you can get an overview of the existing and necessary accessories for commissioning the device. Depending on the intended application, this accessory is very different, since the Raspberry Pi is very flexible.

For example, the Raspberry can be configured with screen output via the existing HDMI output or via the CVBS socket, but also operate without a connected monitor is possible. This is especially useful if the Raspberry is to quietly and unobserved to perform his service, for example, as a controller for a security camera or a doorbell.

In any case, the power supply that is made via a micro USB socket on the Raspberry Pi board is imperative.

Micro USB Cable And Power Supply

Mini vs. Micro: With the almost unmanageable plug and corresponding variety of sockets on the USB port, the Raspberry is in need of the slightly flatter micro USB cable than the mini-mini, which is mainly used in mobile devices such as smartphones and navigation systems. In terms of power supply is for the stable operation of the Raspberry Pi, a 5-W power supply (5 V, 1000 mAh), the right one. Here we have misused the surrounding power supply (5.4 V, 1000 mAh) of a Garmin Nüvi 3790 T since, in our case, this is only used in the car anyway.

Because of the micro-USB port and the low power consumption are especially power supplies from the mobile phone accessories market.

When buying a similar power supply can be so quoted around 5 euros - preferably in a communication dealer as niebauer.com who also useful additions such as fast SD memory cards, Bluetooth mobile keyboards also be used for the Raspberry Pi let mini-screens etc. has in his assortment. So, if something should not work, you have the advantage of being able to make representations there immediately - including exchanges -; in the case of an anonymous provider via the Internet, the e-mails will only be sent back and forth.

Screen And Raspberry: HDMI, CVBS or Nothing

For connection to a screen, the Raspberry Pi offers an HDMI connection and, alternatively, a so-called CVBS connection. Depending on the intended application purpose, the operation without a connected screen is possible, such as for the control of a bell system or video surveillance, etc., if the Raspberry Pi should finally do tax or control tasks.

Apart from multimedia use via OpenELEC, where the Raspberry Pi is directly connected to the TV via HDMI connection, the Raspberry Pi is perfectly suited for background services such as AirPrint, AirPlay, etc. and comes here without screen and keyboard.

Whereas powerful computers used to be housed in a sturdy metal cage with low-noise fans, today's generation of minicomputers, such as the Raspberry Pi, comes without any active fans and is even sold without a housing. But just for visual reasons, the purchase of a suitable housing makes sense. Other offerings such as passive heat sinks for the Raspberry Pi, on the other hand, recall the days of the cheapest backyard workshop, when the computers were still assembled cheaply by self-appointed specialists.

Long story short: save the money and invest it better in a matching power supply. For a new Raspberry Pi costs just under 34 euros, the heatsink with 8 euros plus shipping amount to more than a quarter of the price. Even if the seller here promises an increase in performance in the description text, the question arises, where the well should come from - as well as the question of the quality of the adhesive film, especially if one remembers the dangling processor fans in earlier PC times.

Raspberry Pi: DIY In Two Minutes

Depending on the purpose and personal preference, the small, check-card-sized Raspberry Pi board is operated by the hard-core without any protection in the form of a housing, etc. Depending on the location of the board and possible weather conditions, this is not only not advisable, but a housing may even be mandatory. Be responsible enough and use a suitably sized and safe solution for your application. The Raspberry Pi Forum, in particular and the Internet, in general, abound, providing ideas and examples of DIY or assembling a case. It only takes a little time and creativity to create a personal gem for the Raspberry Pi.

The Case: Build Yourself Or Buy

If you do not have a creative self-builder, you can use the junk-zone of the internet in the auction houses and look for a fitting case from the numerous providers. Here, pay particular attention to the type designation for the Raspberry Pi case - although the Raspberry Pi models are almost identical, but the number of connections varies depending on the model A / B1 / B2, and this also affects the case and the jacks out. It can be assumed that the successor models are similarly compact and clearly designed.

Basically, the Raspberry Pi can be operated without housing due to the small and robust design. However, depending on the purpose and location, you should still think about the use of a housing - especially when the Raspberry Pi is placed in the living room on the TV, and small children's fingers in the household go on a journey of discovery.

Plexiglas Housing For Easy Mating

You get dirt cheap housing in the market - there is no doubt about that. Like everything else in the world, a decent case has its price. This starts with the look: the cheaper a case is, the more boring it usually looks. The choice of the right housing depends mainly on the purpose and of course on the price. Basically, the prettier and the better the processing, the higher the price. For a good compromise in terms of price and appearance, in this case, provide transparent Plexiglas plates.

Good housings for the Raspberry Pi have a lot to offer in terms of ease of assembly. The PCB is then clamped in a housing holder, which you simply put together for easier assembly and which also makes a robust impression otherwise.

With the Plexiglas solutions for the Raspberry Pi, you have to deal a little more gently with the clamp closures, because a leg is broken off quickly. This is not bad at first, because there are three more that hold the case together. But you should not disassemble and assemble the housing too often. This is usually not necessary because the better housing the Raspberry Pi ports cut out accordingly, and thus they can be used comfortably.

Creative And Colorful: Lego Housing From The Toy Box

If there is still a box of Lego bricks left in the basement of the son, and if dusting away, the purchase of the Raspberry Pi is an opportunity to knock down the dust from the box and build a suitable housing with the existing Lego bricks.

Here you can let your creativity run free: When assembling the Lego bricks simply the places for the respective connections - power supply, depending on the application USB and / or LAN or HDMI / CVBS output for connecting the screen - off.

Chapter 2 - Setting Up And Configuring Raspberry Pi

After assembling the Raspberry Pi and refueling the SD card with the desired image for the new »computer,« it is put into operation. Before you go ahead and place the SD card in the Raspberry Pi, you should at least know the configuration parameters for the Raspberry Pi in order to tailor the small minicomputer to the intended purpose. The configuration parameters are defined in the text file config.txt, which is located in the boot directory of the Linux distribution used. After switching on the Raspberry Pi via the power cable, it is read at system startup and interpreted accordingly. If, for example, no screen is used on the Raspberry Pi, this should also be set accordingly in the config.txt file.

No Screen Connected? - Fix Boot Problems

No sound after switching on the power cord? The case occurred when the first start of the Raspberry Pi when it came to take this without a connected screen in operation. During the initial setup you should connect a USB keyboard, and a screen to at least enable the SSH server function. This allows the Raspberry Pi to be conveniently remotely administered with the computer via SSH.

Open this file directly on the memory card and use a Unix-compatible text editor that works correctly in terms of line breaks and character encoding. While you can handle onboard resources from Unix-based operating systems such as Mac OS X, you better use editors like Notepad ++, Primalscript, or UltraEdit, which are all highly recommended. Here you look in the file for a possible culprit - in practice, once for the

HDMI screen, output changes are necessary if no screen is to be connected. In this case the option hdmi_force_hotplug = 1 has to be set - in this case comment out.

SD Cards: The Difference Between Fast And Slow

If the Raspberry Pi still does not start, you should take the used SD card out of the Raspberry Pi and inspect it more closely. The reason: not every SD card can be used with the Raspberry Pi with any operating system - here; there are different experiences.

If you read on the Internet in numerous forums on the subject of Raspberry Pi, you have the impression that the selection of the right SD card is a game of luck nowadays: Here is the widespread opinion that you can minimize the risk of a bad buy only then if you avoid the faster cards, which usually have capacities larger than 16 GB.

In addition to the classic SD cards with capacities from 8 MB to 2 GB, there are cards that either use the SDHC technology (SD 2.0) with capacities from 4 GB to 32 GB or the SDXC technology (SD 2.0) with capacities between 48 GByte and a maximum of 2TB are equipped.

For the Raspberry Pi, especially the SDHC cards come into question - not least for cost reasons. Basically, SDHC cards are divided into different speed classes, which are also printed on the cards. That is, a class 6 labeled SD card has a write speed of at least 6 MB per second. In contrast, the reading speed can not be determined directly from the speed class. In most cases, it is well above the specified minimum write speed, and higher-end models usually achieve higher read speeds than lower-rated SD cards.

The use or selection of the correct SD card depends primarily on the intended use of the Raspberry Pi: In our case, we set a Class 10 for the Raspberry Pi in connection with the OpenELEC project Sandisk Extreme with 16 GB, which has been in continuous operation for three months.

On another Raspberry Pi, which provides network services on the home network, however, is a slower 8 GB Class 4 card in use. For the use of the Raspberry Pi with a space-heavy Zoneminder installation, however, an 8 GB card is again the minimum - but here you have many directories and data outside the SD card, for example, the USB port, to a USB port. Stick or reconfigured on network shares; this can be more than sufficient again.

Select Image and Install on SD Card

The speed check is particularly useful if you have several flash memory, speak SD cards, available, all in terms of capacity for the Raspberry Pi are sufficient, but you do not know which of them is the fastest. Since the published operating system images for the Raspberry Pi require a 2 GByte card and therefore hold correspondingly large partitions, this size should represent the lowest minimum. The prerequisite for this benchmark are administrator rights under Windows.

For the selection and installation of the appropriate operating system for the Raspberry Pi, the steadily growing network community provides suitable images that you can try free of charge and without obligation. The download addresses of the various operating system images for the Raspberry Pi are listed in the table below.

At first glance, the beginner does not understand what lies behind the respective distribution and multimedia center compilation. Even hardcore, advanced Linux pros find it hard to gauge the differences in XMBC builds. In addition, every user has their own preferences, but with the use of the Raspbian / Debian image on your Raspberry Pi, you will not be wrong at first.

Every few weeks, new versions of the image files are published on the relevant Raspberry Pi pages, such as www.raspberrypi.org - in this example; we used the Wheezy-Raspian package dated 16.08.2012. This can be later updated during operation in a few moments - the downloading and installing the image on the SD memory card is, therefore, a one-time thing.

Commissioning: Root Or Pi?
If the operating system is freshly installed and no keyboard and language customizations have yet been made, the initial login will be done with the default user and default password, which varies depending on the operating system used.

If, for example, the SSH server on the Raspberry Pi is initially deactivated, a direct login to the Raspberry Pi is also possible, provided that a keyboard and a screen are connected.

Because of the default US keyboard, the letter "y" of the raspberry password on the connected German keyboard is still on the letter "z." In this case, use the password raspberry. No matter which image or operating system you use - after logging in to the Raspberry Pi for the first time, you change the password of the user with the password command, which ensures greater security during operation.

Windows: The USB Image Tool In Use
A similarly convenient command-line tool as dd from the Unix world is unfortunately not available for Windows. To transfer

the image file to the SD card under Windows, the USB Image Tool is available here. The tool itself requires the DotNet (.Net) environment under Windows, which should also be installed on a state-of-the-art Windows system. If not, you must first download and install .Net from Microsoft to get the USB Image Tool up and running can.

Backup With The USB Image Tool

After starting the program, select the USB drive in the left-hand pane and click on the backup button in the lower right corner. Note that the memory size of the memory card backup naturally also corresponds to the capacity of the inserted card. This may be a problem with memory cards larger than 4 GB if the backup is to be stored on an old file system.

Transfer Image To The SD Card

For example, to write the downloaded Raspian image to the inserted SD card data carrier, the Admin mode is also required under Windows. If you have not already done so, start the USB Image Tool in Admin mode by highlighting the file and using the context menu of the right mouse button to select Run as administrator. Then select the extracted operating system image of the Raspian system by clicking on the Restore button.

After writing the image file, do not remove the memory card yet, first quit the USB Image Tool, and then safely remove the hardware. There, select the SD card data carrier or the corresponding drive and end the operation of the SD card by clicking on the OK button.

SD cards are now available in countless different capacity and speed classes, and meanwhile, more or less 4 or 8 GB SD cards are standard equipment. For compatibility and especially for space reasons, the Raspberry makers provide the appropriate Debian / Raspian image in the (unpacked) size of 2 GB, which, as described above, also on a larger memory card with 4, 8 or

16 GB can be transferred.

No Witchcraft: Fdisk In Use

In the first step, you select the used memory card - in this case it is device mmcblk0. Use the following command to enter the fdisk command mode:

sudo fdisk / dev / mmcblk0

Now you are in your own fdisk console. Entering the letter m gives you an overview of the available commands at any time.

Now let's start by outputting the current parameters of the installed memory card with the command p:

Now the two available partitions are displayed on the SD memory card. Here is the order of the sectors, which are counted in ascending order. The Raspberry Pi image has a fixed FAT32 portion (from sector 8192 to 122879) mounted as the / boot partition, as well as the actual Linux partition that begins immediately after sector 122880.

The goal is, therefore, to enlarge the Linux partition. This is where the FAT32 partition remains, the Linux partition is first deleted and recreated with the old sector start limit. The value of the end sector, of course, depends on the new size - but more on that later. First, delete the Linux partition of the memory card.

Deleting And Creating Partitions

They do not really erase the data, just change the partition limits for the memory card. In this example, there are two partitions. The second partition is the Linux partition. For deletion, in this example, first, enter the letter command d (delete) followed by the partition statement 2.

In the next step, you enter the new partition limit for the Linux partition.

When creating a new partition, first tell fdisk with the n command that you want to create a new partition. Since this is a so-called primary partition, then enter the associated command p for it. The partition number is calculated automatically, but can also be adjusted. In this example, the same number 2 is used for the partition number as for the already used Linux partition.

Checking And Partitioning The SD Card

On the one hand, you take over the partition limits from the "old" Linux partition - because you left the first partition unchanged, the boot sector of the second partition remains the same as 122880. To specify the end sector of the second partition, use the default entry, which depends on the available memory card size. In this example, this is the value 7744511 - which here corresponds to the full capacity of the 4 GB SD card.

Save And Activate Partitions

Now, the changes to the partition limits have been entered in the fdisk console but not yet activated and saved. This is done with the w (write) command - but if you do not want to save the changes made, use the q (quit) command to exit the fdisk console.

After exiting the fdisk console, you start with the command and sudo reboot the Raspberry Pi new. If necessary, the file system must be rearranged and repaired after the restart so that this, too, can handle the changed capacity.

Adjust The File System Again

After rebooting the Raspberry Pi and logging into the console, use the Resize2fs command to customize the file system:
sudo resize2fs -p / dev / mmcblk0p2
The 2-parameter -p used in the example is used to display the progress bar when customizing the file system.
At the end of the procedure, check on the console whether the memory space on the Raspberry Pi has really grown: Use the command df -h to list the memory space of the active

partitions.

The capacity specification for rootfs or / dev / root is informative: In this case, you should have nearly double the capacity in the case of a 4 GB SD card.

Tuning Measures For The Raspberry Pi

After a while, any computer is too slow, including the Raspberry Pi. But with the Raspberry Pi you have the disadvantage that you can not simply add additional memory or a faster CPU - the compact design makes a hardware-side expansion impossible , What remains are the interventions in the Kernel and operating system beginnings, also the optimization of the Linux file system can bring here a few percent additional resources. In effect , how fast the Raspberry Pi will feel depends on the purpose and amount of services and programs installed on the Raspberry Pi. However, the tips below provide for performance enhancements here and there.

Overview Of System Utilization With htop

Before you blindly and luckily make any system or configuration changes, you should first learn in principle, where the bottleneck is in the system: With the appropriate tool, you will learn which processes how many resources need. Then you can decide whether you want to run one or the other program instead of another computer or even install additional services and programs, should there still be enough CPU time and memory available. If not already available, install the tool htop by command:

sudo apt-get install htop

After starting htop, the memory and CPU-intensive processes are listed in descending order. Depending on the service in progress, the information is constantly changing, but for a basic assessment this is more than sufficient: If a process over a longer period, for example, a continuous CPU time of over 90%, either the Raspberry is too weak, or the process is On the best way to operate the Raspberry Pi at the stop. Here, if necessary, the reconfiguration of the memory allocation of the Raspberry Pi will help.

Optimization By Memory Splitting

Basically, the file start.elf specifies the distribution of the total memory available on the Raspberry Pi between main and graphics memory for the operating system. After the basic installation, Debian / Raspian's / boot directory contains different files with the extension * .elf. No matter how many of them are in the directory - only the file start.elf is used and evaluated when starting the operating system. By default, this is configured for a Raspberry Pi with a total of 256 MByte on an allocation of 192 MB of memory for the RAM and 64 MB for the graphics memory (Debian).

Then there are 224 MB available for the main memory (RAM) for which Video memory (GPU) 32 MB. After rebooting, the Raspberry Pi is the changed division then active.

If you have a Raspberry model with 512 MB of total memory in use, you can also change the allocation:

RAM graphics VRAM use case 256 MB 256 MByte GUI usage, many applications with video features, Playing and decoding, streaming, XBMC, mandatory for Full HD 1920 playback.

384 MB 128 MByte GUI usage, many applications with video capabilities, Playing and decoding, streaming, XBMC, mandatory for Full HD 1920 playback.

448 MB 64 MByte In principle, no GUI usage recommended, no playback videos, no hardware video acceleration, exclusively providing network services.

496 MB 16 MB Absolutely no GUI usage is recommended as well as none playing videos, no hardware video acceleration, exclusively providing network services.

Since October 2012, the allocation of memory via the corresponding files is a thing of the past. These are then no longer available in the / boot directory - only the well-known files start.elf, and start_cd.elf as well as fixup * .elf are allowed with the new firmware. Here the distribution is controlled by a parameter in the configuration file config.txt. By specifying gpu_mem = 16 assigns the graphics memory size of 16 MB. The values permitted here are between 16 and 192 MB for a 256 MB RAM Raspberry, and for the 512 MB model the permissible range is 16 to 448 MB. The rest of the memory not allocated to the graphics card is automatically used as RAM memory.

Command Line Fetishists: Stop GUI Startup

Depending on the operating system used on the Raspberry Pi, you have a different approach. Basically, you use the raspi-config command to set the basic installation of the Raspberry Pi . Here you check that the switch boot_behaviourstart desktop on boot? set to No. If you would like to start the graphical X11 interface later from the text-based terminal, simply do so via the command startx in the console.

If so, modify it to use the execute privilege per sudo chmod 644 /etc/init.d/slim remove, or remove the slim package completely from the Raspberry Pi with the command sudo apt-get purge slim.

Support Memory: Create Swap File

Especially for systems with a small amount of memory, the setup of a so-called paging file or a paging memory brings a big plus in performance. Especially when many services and programs are active, they require more memory than physically available. For example, in order for the operating system to operate flexibly, Linux does not work directly with the physical RAM, but rather with the virtual main memory, which consists of the physical RAM and a defined memory area on the hard disk. Here, the virtual memory on the hard disk is provided by the swap partition or as a swap file.

To create a so-called swap file on the Raspberry Pi, open a file and use the dd command to write in as many bytes as the swap file should be large. The swap file must then be formatted with the mkswap command. Finally, activation takes place in the system via swapon command.

In the next step, you integrate the created swap file into the file system of the Raspberry Pi. This requires an intervention in the system file fstab.

Configure Swap File In Fstab

Basically, you will find in the / etc / fstab file all volumes or the corresponding partitions that should be automatically mounted when the Raspberry Pi starts up. To open and edit this file, root privileges are necessary. With the command
sudo bash

nano / etc / fstab

Open the configuration file and comment out the / var / swapfile entry if it already exists in the fstab file. In this case, remove the leading picket fence icon (#). If the entry does not yet exist, enter it - the spaces between the entries / values are set using the [Tab] key.

Since the fstab file is currently open on this occasion, you can also stop saving the access time of a file or to a directory on the Raspberry Pi, which can bring a small burst of speed.

Optimize Files And Directories Via Fstab

The data partition of the SD card is also entered in the fstab file so that it is available to the operating system after starting the Raspberry Pi. Here you also add the nodiratime parameter in the line after the defaults, noatime entry. Basically, it is by default that Linux stores the last access time of a file (atime). For Raspberry Pi use this information is usually not needed - even the time of accessing a directory is uninteresting, which can bring here a small burst of speed.

After the change, you save the file, but the tuning action will be active after the restart of the Raspberry Pi.

Reduce Consoles

For miser: If you want to further optimize in terms of storage needs, turn off the file a few more consoles - usually no more than two are needed. Open the file for this

sudo nano / etc / inittab

and comment there with the picket fence symbol (#) the getties 2 to 6:

Chapter 3 - Step By Step To The Perfect System

If you want to put a perfectly tuned Raspberry Pi into operation in your home network, you can configure your system as it is necessary after installation. Since the Raspberry Pi does not have a BIOS or EFI compared to a computer, it works with configuration files and many parameters. Therefore, it is necessary to learn something and apply different Linux commands in the console. This is the only way to directly influence the existing programs and services, the customization of the language settings and the keyboard, but also later to set up the network and much more.

Customize Console Settings

If the Raspberry Pi does not display a configuration menu after the first start, you can do so by entering

sudo raspi-config

Start manually to make the initial setup. If you have loaded the American keyboard driver, you must use the [ß] key instead of the hyphen key since the wrong keyboard setting is currently active. After starting raspi-config, navigate with the arrow keys and the [Tab] key in the text-based user interface. First, adjust the console settings and set here via the menu item the default settings of the localization.

If the terminal is now converted to the German language and the UTF-8 encoding, check the set keyboard layout of the Raspberry Pi. In the main menu of raspi-config, select the item configure_keyboard. If you connect to the Raspberry Pi mainly via SSH, the selection of the keyboard tur Generic 105-key (Intl) PC recommended.

To change the keyboard layout to QWERTZ, select Other in

the following dialog to go to the language selection. There you navigate with the arrow keys to the entry German and select the OK entry with the [Tab] key.

In the subsequent dialog, select German again, and after confirming with OK, a dialog will appear in which you can define the function of the [Alt_Gr] key on the keyboard. Here, as well as in the configuration of the so-called ComposeKey, you keep the default settings.

Last but not least, you can use the keyboard shortcuts [Ctrl] + [Alt] + [Back] as a key combination to quit the X server. Make sure the switch boot_behaviour start desktop on boot? set to No. If you would like to start the graphical X11 interface from the text-based terminal later, simply use the command startx in the console.

Adjust Console Settings

For the changes to take effect, quit the raspi-config menu by choosing Finish and start in the following dialog on Would you like to reboot now? by selecting Yes, the Raspberry Pi new. If you want to reboot later, you can do so with the command

sudo reboot

If the US keyboard on the Raspberry is active again after the reboot, check the settings of the configured keyboard with the command

sudo dpkg-reconfigure keyboard-configuration

To subsequently make changes to the localization and time zone on the console, you can use the commands

sudo dpkg-reconfigure tzdata

sudo dpkg-reconfigure console-setup

use to directly start the appropriate configuration.

Console Basics: Important Commands At A Glance

The console or, in the case of Linux and Mac OS, the terminal comes in text mode by default and can also be started from the window manager. So that Linux newbies also feel right at home on the command line, here are the most important commands at a glance:

Description command

Ends the specified running kill process

Execute command as superuser sudo [COMMAND]

Change user usermod [USER]

Add Users useradd [USER]

Delete user userdel [USER]

Copy file cp [filename.extension] [TARGET] /

Delete file mv [filename.extension]

Find file find -name "[filename.extension]"

Move file mv [filename.extension] [TARGET] /

Show file content less [filename.extension]

Services on the Raspberry Pi terminate service [service name] stop

Services on the Raspberry Pi start service [service name] start

Restart services on the Raspberry Pi service [service name] restart

Find out DNS information host

Editor nano nano [path] [filename]

Ctrl key and X to save and exit

Editor vi vi [path] [filename]

Esc key and: q to save

i-key for changing / inserting text

Creates links between files and folders ln

Show free space df -h

Unpack GZ archive gunzip [filename.gz]

Help on individual commands man [COMMAND]

Stop running processes and shut down the system shut down

Show list of active processes ps -ax

List of previously entered commands history

Show

Description command

Find MAC address arp -a

Display network configuration ifconfig

Delete folder rmdir [FOLDER NAME]

Change Folder cd / [FOLDER NAME]

Show folder contents ls or ls -al

Change password passwd

SSH connection to remote computer ssh [IP address] or:

take ssh [DNS address]

When changing user the desired user names before [IP address] or [DNS

Address]: ssh_benutzername @ [IP address]

Unzip TGZ archive tar xzvf [filename.tgz]

Shows the current location in the lwd folder

Displays the hostname to hostname

Displays the path of a program

For more information about a command, it's best to use the man mechanism. With the man command (from manual, manual), the console throws out the appropriate syntax with parameters for almost every console command. For example, typing cp will list all the parameters for copying the file / folder.

Chmod: Effective Permissions

A specialty in Unix, in general, is the chmod command. The Unix rights system has three different areas:

• user
• Group (group)
• Other (other)

The following properties can be assigned for each area:
• r = readable, value: 4
• w = writable, value: 2
• x = executable (executable), value: 1
On the Linux of the Raspberry Pi, for example, if you run ls, properties are displayed in the following format:
rwxrwxrwx
The first three letters are for the user domain, another three are group, and the last three are for other. To get the representation in the form of an octal number, you have to add all values for each range. In this case: (4 + 2 + 1) (4) (4) = 744. So you can use
chmod 744 [FILENAME.DATE EXTENSION]
set the appropriate rights.

Chapter 4 - Raspberry In The Network

If you want to bring the Raspberry Pi in the home network and the Internet, it must be a cable to the distributor (router) shot. If this is not the case, you can also create a network connection by radio. All you need is a suitable WLAN adapter for the Raspberry Pi.

It does not matter which network interface you are using, by default, the Raspberry Pi has a DHCP client active that obtains its network parameters from the Dynamic Host Configuration Protocol (DHCP) server in your home network. Not only does DHCP provide the IP address, but it also lets you automatically set preferences for the DNS server, gateway, netmask, domain, and more with the help of options.

The IP address of the Raspberry Pi can be assigned statically but dynamically, depending on the MAC address of the computer. In short, the Raspberry Pi gets its IP address and associated network settings assigned automatically.

Control Raspberry Pi via SSH: PuTTY, Terminal & Co. In Use

Particularly secure access to Unix-based systems is not only possible via a so-called secure, encrypted connection, but also urgently recommended over the Internet for security reasons. Access via the WLAN interface is even more so. Thus, not only is the WLAN generally safer thanks to a secure router configuration with the use of WPA / WPA2, but also the access via SSH provides additional security so that unauthorized persons can not make nonsense on the target computer. Once SSH access is set up, you can access the system and user data on the target computer, copy data back and forth, and much more, depending on the user.

Practical And Secure: Access Via SSH

A Raspberry Pi does not require peripherals such as a mouse, keyboard, or screen to operate, and because of its flexibility, it is also of great interest for out-of-the-ordinary places. If you want to administrate comfortably from the desk or the sofa, you will appreciate the SSH functionality. This makes it possible to get the remote command line on the local computer as if you were sitting directly in the garage in front of a connected screen with a keyboard.

After the Raspberry Pi has been switched on for the first time, a configuration dialog appears, in which the start of the SSH server can be lashed so that it is available after each power-on. Then you can connect to any client over the network using the secure SSH protocol with the Raspberry Pi.

Debian Squeeze: Turn On SSH

The choice of operating system with the Raspberry Pi depends mainly on the future purpose and the associated functions: For example, who instead of Debian Wheezy (Debian 7) still uses the predecessor Debian Squeeze (Debian 6) can easily in the first partition of the SD Reboot the boot_enable_ssh.rc file in boot.rc to turn on SSH functionality (FAT32 / boot partition).

After plugging into the Raspberry Pi, the built-in SSH server is activated and can now be accessed as usual via the home network with a suitable SSH client. Some operating systems not only bring a built-in SSH client, but also a built-in SSH server, and then it is possible to access non-Unix- based operating systems like Windows. However, this also requires the installation of an SSH client.

No Installation Required: Windows Access Via PuTTY

If you have not already done so: Download an SSH client program to the Windows PC for secure access to the

Mac. PuTTY is a real pleasure for purists of the command line, who would rather work in the window world, for which stands with WinSCP (www.winscp.com/), a suitable tool at the disposal.

Practical And Clear: Switch On PuTTY Full-Screen Mode

Especially in the beginning, when setting up the Raspberry Pi you work a lot on the console until the Raspberry Pi is set up as far as you wish. Especially when restarting PuTTY, it is annoying to constantly set the window to the desired size with the mouse - here, the full-screen display is much more useful. These can be used with the key combination [Alt] + [Enter] with activated PuTTY and thus also back to the window mode.

[Alt] + [Enter] is not activated, you can also start the PuTTY full-screen mode by right-clicking on the title bar of the terminal window.

To enable full-screen mode by default, select the Behavior entry in the left pane of PuTTY when it is started and then activate Full screen on Alt-Enter. If this is not only valid for the current, but also for all other terminal windows in the future, save the setting in the Session area. There, under Load, save or delete a stored session, select the entry Default Settings and then click the Save button.

For an existing saved session, however, the customization does not count. Here you must first load the corresponding profile, activate the key combination as described above, and then save the profile again.

Switch Off Raspberry Pi With A Mouse Click

On the above download page of PuTTY you will also find an additional program called plink.exe. You place this in the same directory in which the program putty.exe is already stored. In the example below, both the putty.exe file and the plink.exe file are located in the C: \ directory of the Windows hard disk.

echo off

c: \ plink.exe -ssh -pw openelec root@192.168.123.47 poweroff

exit

Then save the file with a descriptive name and the file extension .cmd. The file can also be stored in the same directory as the PuTTY tools - this requires a desktop link to the cmd batch file. Alternatively, create the cmd file directly on the Windows desktop. Now save yourself from logging in and shutting down the Raspberry Pi.

Mac OS X: SSH Access Through The Built-In Console

Unlike Windows, the SSH client is already included in Mac OS X. So only the opening of a terminal window via Programs / Utilities / Terminal is necessary, then can be by command

ssh root @ IP ADDRESS

to access the target computer. After entering the password, the file system of the remote station is available. For those who prefer a bit more convenience, get the freeware Cyberduck, which lets you drag and drop files and entire directories from the Mac to the target computer.

Before connecting, configure Cyberduck with the SFTP protocol and input the IP address of the Raspberry Pi on the server. Alternatively, if configured, use the DNS name of the remote site. The default SSH port setting is 22 and does not need to be changed. For username, you use the account that is available to you for the target computer - if password is the corresponding password.

Retrofit WLAN Adapter: Attention, Chipset!

Once the SSH access has been successfully established, you can switch and act as you wish: The main area of application via the SSH console is the remote maintenance of the target computer, which can now not only be accomplished quickly but also thanks to the encryption used goes.

Ubuntu: Retrofit SSH Access

Similar to Mac OS X, the SSH client is usually included on Linux systems. But sometimes it comes with extremely slim configured Linux derivatives that it must be installed after.

New operating systems adapted for the Raspberry Pi have included built-in kernel driver support for USB WLAN adapters since October 2012, based on the Realtek chipset (RTL8188CUS and others).

If you are planning to use a WLAN adapter on the Raspberry Pi, you should make sure that it is equipped with a Realtek chip - the RTL8188CUS - when purchasing the WLAN adapter.

Here you can then use the plug-in card without further ado and configure it directly with the appropriate WLAN tools or the configuration parameters via the network setting of the Raspberry Pi. Basically, with the Komman-dos lsusb and dmesg you can find out which devices are currently active on the USB bus.

When using lsusb -v, the built-in chip is usually also displayed in the WLAN adapter. If not, you can continue to research using the device ID - which comes in the 1234: 1234 format.

Download And Install Driver

On the other hand, if you do not want to or do not want to switch to a new firmware or operating system, you can still install the WLAN USB port manually. After restarting the Raspberry Pi, restart the script:

After the actual driver installation, which is done automatically by the script, the network settings for the wireless network have to be defined.

With Certainty: Defining Network Settings

After integrating the WLAN interface in the Linux configuration - here it is available as an interface under wlan0 - this must be configured. Here, the script inter alia queries the SSID and the access password for the wireless router, if access to it (hopefully) secured by a secure WPA2 password.

After selecting the encryption method, enter the name of the SSID to be used. These entries can be adjusted later if necessary and are stored in the network / interfaces. The script then scans the WLAN environment and searches for the appropriate wireless network.

If the network parameters are entered correctly and the wireless network is initialized correctly, these parameters are saved.

Commissioning WLAN

Now the script has come to an end, as it were - you still have the choice, whether the Raspberry Pi should be brought up to date in terms of operating system and firmware or not. Select this option, but you may need to re-run the WLAN configuration after rebooting the Raspberry Pi to keep it enabled.

After using the easy system and operating system update option of the script after the WLAN driver installation and configuration, the setup WLAN may not be available after restarting the Raspberry Pi.

You simply check this in the console with the command ifconfig, which then outputs all active network interfaces. If the entry wlan0 is missing here, the following workaround helps for one-off users:

After the update, start the installation script for the WLAN adapter again and navigate through the individual points. All you need to do is to confirm or skip the parameters already set, such as SSID, encryption, etc. Also, the start of the system and operating system updates are not necessary. Run the script to the end - until the command prompt is available again in the console. Afterward, the WLAN configuration is saved and is available again after a restart of the Raspberry Pi. Pull the LAN cable before the WLAN stick test. If the WLAN does not work, this usually has a trivial reason. So if you want to try out your WLAN stick, you should pull the LAN cable before starting the Raspberry Pi.

Just to run the Raspberry Pi on the net and use it to surf the web with multiple computers or from the couch, a home network would be a shame. You'll quickly see how convenient it is to share data between multiple computers, print jobs from one central printer, share digital photos with everyone on the net, and more. This is all feasible with onboard resources. Also, safety aspects are not too short. However, you need a few basic requirements for smooth operation. In order to exchange data in the home network with other computers, the following prerequisites are necessary:

• TCP / IP installed.
• Working group established.
• Computer name entered.
• One or more computers have at least one folder or drive shared.
• Shutter names without umlauts, special characters and spaces, and no more than twelve characters.

For this to work, in addition to the IP configuration of the DSL router, the network parameters must be properly installed on each computer. This means in plain text that on each computer, a network adapter (network card, AirPort / WLAN card, etc.) is present and installed.

DHCP: IP Address Searched

When the Raspberry Pi is freshly unpacked and installed, its network interface is configured by default for DHCP (Dynamic Host Configuration Protocol) access. DHCP has its advantages, especially in large networks. This means that all computers connected to the router, regardless of whether they are WLAN or not, are automatically assigned the TCP / IP configuration. Manufacturers usually recommend not to change these settings and to use the domestic DSL / WLAN router as a DHCP server. DHCP, the dynamic allocation of IP addresses in the network, is both a blessing and a curse.

First of all, it is practical for every network newcomer not to have to worry about assigning such IP addresses.

If you have only a few computers to supply you with your router, it is often more sensible and safer to disable the DHCP server in the wireless router and manually configure the connected clients. Not only do you have an accurate overview of which computer is on the network with which IP address, but also make it more difficult for a potential intruder to "grab" an IP address in your home network.

If there is no DHCP server or DSL router in the network that is responsible for the automatic assignment of the IP addresses, the IP addresses and the subnet masks must be entered manually for each computer. The choice of the IP address is up to you. For a better overview, you should always ascending an address with 192.168.123.1, 192.168.123.2, etc. awarded.

In a home network, the Raspberry Pi is usually integrated with the Ethernet interface. Friends of wireless pleasure use Wi-Fi via a small Wi-Fi adapter, which they still have to get extra. No matter which of the two ways you go, the IP configuration is almost identical for both interfaces. Despite DHCP, you can also reserve an IP address for a computer in the LAN by selecting DHCP with manual address.

This will always give this computer the same IP address when accessing the DHCP server. This is particularly the case with highly available computers and servers, which often require permanent IP settings, for example, because port forwarding is active in the DSL / WLAN router - this has also proven to be extremely favorable for the Raspberry Pi in practice.

Accessing The Raspberry Pi File System Via The Home Network

Anyone who has a Mac or a Windows computer in their home network, in addition to the Raspberry Pi will eventually want to transport data from A to B and back. To access the Raspberry Pi file system or individual directories conveniently from home computers the installation and configuration of the Samba package is necessary. Samba is included in almost every Linux distribution; it only needs to be selected during installation.

With Samba, the Raspberry Pi behaves like a Windows server for the computers on the network. If Samba is optimally configured, you can later create your own log-in profiles for all users and user groups. These are then stored in a directory on the Raspberry Pi and exported as a / netlogon directory. The Windows clients then automatically use the appropriate log-in scripts. Basically, you can copy the contents of the file printed here. Only the global entries for netbios name, server string, and workgroup should be adjusted.

First, create the smb.conf file that controls the Samba configuration for the Samba configuration. This belongs to the Raspberry Pi with Debian in the directory / etc / samba and has several blocks, each containing variables for configuration can be set. Each block represents a release in principle, with two areas of particular importance. The most important of these is the [global] section that sets the general Samba settings.

In the [homes] section, a user who accesses the Raspberry / Debian server from another computer is provided with the home directory on request. This requires an entry in the smbpasswd file. Via smbpasswd -a NAME, create a Samba user in the / etc / smbpasswd file:
sudo smbpasswd -a pi

Now enter the password of the user pi and confirm it. Subsequently, this user can be used under Samba. This admittedly unfriendly double administration effort for the user passwords, you can turn off with a small intrusion into the smb.conf:
unix password sync = yes
However, the most important entries are already present in the printed smb.conf.
With the command ps fax | grep smbd check if the samba server is really running. If not, you may find a typo or syntax error in the smb.conf file. With the Samba test program testparm you can easily and safely check the Samba configuration for possible errors.
Fortunately, if the testparm program issues error messages, it also indicates the line number of the line in which the error most likely occurred. In this case, please correct the corresponding lines in the smb.conf file. If the configuration goes through, you have made the first part, congratulations! To be on the safe side, restart the Samba daemon:
sudo service samba restart
If you already have a computer in the home network in

operation, you can see the Raspberry Pi in the network environment after restarting the Samba service. Now check the Samba user configuration on the computer.

Afterward, the corresponding shares are visible in the Explorer. If you wish, you can assign a separate drive letter to the network drive under Win-dows using the command Map network drive.

Now you can access the Raspberry Pi from all computers in the home network - of course, that is also possible.

Pair Mac OS X with Raspberry Pi via Samba

If you do not want to go the cumbersome way via an FTP / HTTP server in the home network, you better use the direct route via a Windows share as described above. But the reverse approach, namely accessing the Raspberry Pi to a configured Mac share, is also possible after some setup work on the Mac.

1. In the first step, make sure that the workgroup name of all machines in the network is the same. On the Mac, you open the System Settings Network and here the WINS tab. In the current example, the workgroup is called workgroup first.

2. Another basic requirement is that the corresponding checkmark in File Sharing is set via System Settings / Sharing. The Device Name input box displays the NetBIOS name of the Mac computer that you set in the System Preferences Network on the WINS tab.

3. To configure Windows-to-Mac communication, first make sure the user names are the same on Windows and Mac OS. Here also on request, click on Create a new user account on the plus icon with just a few clicks, which can be used to access the folder to be shared.

4. The New person window appears. Input the user name and the corresponding password. Click on Create account to create

the Mac user.

Ideally, you will use the same password as on Windows - in this case, you will save yourself the hassle of password access on Windows.

In order for the logon or the access from a Windows PC to work, a corresponding directory for access must be defined in the user settings of the user active under Mac OS X, here the directory Public.

5. By default, Mac OS X initially supports only Apple's proprietary Apple Filing Protocol (AFP) for data access to the Mac. In order to grant the Windows world access to the Mac hard disk, you must explicitly allow and set up Windows access here.

In contrast to its predecessors, Mac OS X version 10.5 and higher no longer has the Windows File Sharing switch; the Windows share via Samba is hidden under options in File Sharing. Then select the user account or accounts that are allowed to use Samba access.

6. Last but not least, under Sharing, set the access rights:

7. Now switch to your Windows computer and check the network environment to see if the Mac is visible. If not, restart Windows or press the function key [F5] to refresh the view. Double-click the Mac icon to access the shared Mac directory.

Change NetBIOS Name

The NetBIOS name for the Mac machine is grayed out in the dialog box and can not be changed there. If you want to use a different name, you can change it under System Preferences / Sharing. When the NetBIOS and Workgroup names are configured, the Samba configuration is complete.

When The Mac Denies Access

But for many users, nothing happens. Although the Mac can be seen in the Windows network environment, Windows reports a network error while trying to access it. The solution can be found in the Mac OS X firewall settings. For security reasons, many users have their firewall settings set to allow only necessary services.

1. For Windows to be able to access the Mac, you must enable the option Allow all incoming connections for the first access. The File Sharing service (AFP, SMB) is automatically displayed. After that, you can change the firewall settings again.

2. When you click your Mac icon again in the Windows Network Neighborhood, the Connect to <COMPUTER> dialog box appears. Enter your username and password here. Confirm with OK.

3. The shared Mac directory is displayed in the Windows Explorer, and the flow of data between Mac and Windows - and thus also to the Raspberry Pi - nothing stands in the way of Mac OS side.

Be Careful When Accessing The Macintosh HD

Depending on whether read access and write permissions have been assigned under the system for access, it is important to pay attention here: Since Samba also displays the system folders and files (hidden in Mac OS X) in addition to user data, You should be careful when editing or deleting files. Too big a risk of destroying the user profile on Mac OS X.

Share Windows Folder For Raspberry Pi In The Home Network

The release of a folder under Windows is done in a few clicks: You open the Explorer and select the folder to be shared with other users on the network. Right-click on this folder and in the context menu, right-click Release for. Below is a dialog in which you can set up access to the folder.

Then the configured folder share is active. The user who has been set up for access can now access the set release from another PC in the network - provided that the name and password are set up in the user administration of Windows.

The removal of an established release and a subsequent change are analogous. Here you select the corresponding folder in the Explorer and select Properties or better in the context menu. On the tab Sharing, you get an overview of who can access the folder and which rights or permissions are set up for the different users.

If you would like to remove a created share, deactivate the checkmark in the field Share this folder in the dialog box Extended Release.

Subsequently, access via the network is no longer possible. If the Samba share of the Raspberry Pi becomes a problem when accessing via the Windows Explorer or the directory contents are not displayed, the following tip will help.

Windows Zips When Accessing Samba: Release Problems

If your home network has a Raspberry Pi with Samba, a NAS server (such as QNAP, Buffalo devices), a full-featured Linux / Samba server, and a Samba share for the Mac, accessing the network shares is usually easy if they can be seen in the network environment, and the corresponding access rights are available. That counts only for the first registration.

This annoying issue can be resolved with a small configuration change: Press the Start button, and then you need to type secpol.msc in the Run box. Then go to Local Policies and Security Options, where you can customize the following two entries.

Since neither the group policy editor (gpedit.msc) nor the editor for local security settings (secpol.msc) are included in the functionality of the simple "home user versions" such as Home Basic and Home Premium, you must use the Registry

Editor are gone to the release problems when

Access to the NAS server or the Linux / Samba server in the home network to solve.

Open Network Shares Automatically In The Finder

If you have permanent access to your Raspberry Pi shares in the home network via a Linux / Windows / Samba server, then manually adding the share using the shortcut [Command] + [K] will be annoying over time.

It is more convenient if you automatically connect a shared share and display it in the Finder. Via apple / system settings / user / startup objects, add the desired share (s) as a so-called startup object. First, select the appropriate user, then select Startup Items in the tab and click the Plus icon.

If a password or other user ID, including password is required to access the network share, it is recommended to save the access information in the personal keyring. In this case, the access is established immediately, and the annoying password query is omitted. After the next login, these shares are automatically opened and displayed in a Finder window.

Chapter 5 - Living Room PC 3.0: Smart TV Self-Made

A flexible, powerful, and above all quiet computer in the living room requires special components. The days when chunky computers in mini and midi-tower format were used for smooth, smooth video file playback and Internet / home network access are over. Instead, use the small, fanless Raspberry Pi with the purpose-built OpenELEC system to play all the video and music files from all available video sources in your home network, as well as convenient access to the public Internet TV archives Broadcasters and foreign broadcasters who also publish their broadcasts on the Internet.

Last but not least, you will learn how add-ons can be used to comfortably browse video archives such as Spiegel Online, Süddeutsche.de, and others online and use them free of advertising - all from the comfort of your own couch. The TV broadcasters, in particular, offer a one-of-a-kind program around the clock: Reports, sports, documentaries, reports on current affairs - a completely new viewing experience at the click of a mouse and on-demand. Whenever you want to see the program, it is immediately available.

With the Raspberry Pi in conjunction with Open Embedded Linux Entertainment Center - OpenELEC for short - you have an all-rounder in the living room that retains an overview of all media files in the home and ensures significantly increased comfort and a better selection in everyday TV life.

OpenELEC: Load Or Compile?

If you decide to use OpenELEC, you should also be aware that the installation and configuration of the multimedia functions in the Raspberry Pi are not rocketed science, but require a little time and patience, and above all, the will to occur To understand and solve problems yourself. Of course, advanced users have more options for influencing the configuration and composition of OpenELEC if the package itself - ie the system that comes on the SD card - is compiled and compiled. For those who have little or nothing to do with Linux, Terminal, Shell, and Perl scripts, it is recommended that you download and use a precompiled OpenELEC package.

Download And Customize The OpenELEC Image

No matter what size the image file comes in, it has a compressed file format in the form of a * .tar.gz or * .tar.bz2 file. While unzipping such files on Mac OS or Linux with built-in operating system tools is possible, you need help on Windows. Download the best of the free and completely sufficient for home use Packer 7-zip.

Which operating system image you choose is initially a matter of taste - in principle, of course, best an image file with a relatively fresh build date and - if different sizes for the target SD card are available - the right one to the existing SD card. In this case, you will save yourself from later adapting the OpenELEC installation to the actual capacity of the memory card.

Commissioning A Finished OpenELEC Image

At least during commissioning and initial setup SSH access to the Raspberry Pi system is recommended, but it is disabled by default in OpenELEC. However, SSH can be conveniently switched on when the XBMC is started or by creating an empty file named ssh_enable in the /storage/.config directory become.

Getting, Compiling And Installing OpenELEC

If necessary, insert the memory card into the computer again, mount the memory card in a Unix system and use the

following commands in the terminal window to create the file:
cd /storage/.config
touch ssh_enable

If the card is subsequently plugged into a Raspberry Pi, the SSH server should be started when the OpenELEC is started up. If you have connected to the OpenELEC from a computer via SSH for the first time, change the password of the administrative root user (default: openelec) with a passwd command.

Basically, a real native Linux is recommended for compiling - just for speed and time reasons. If you do not want to have full-fledged native Linux on your computer, you can also prepare and run the installation on Mac OS or Windows using a virtual machine. Basically, you need a reasonably current Linux distribution, so you get the OpenELEC package compiled clean. There are a few special features in the game. As the target platform of the Raspberry Pi is known to be an arm processor architecture, the compiler on the Linux machine must dominate the so-called Cross-Compiling. In this example, we use an Ubuntu installation in a VMware virtual machine.

Preparing To Compile

In the example described below, we used an Ubuntu installation (12.04) under VMware Workstation 8 with the standard configuration. You need hard disk space for the translation - and that's not too tight: you should at least be able to provide around 9 GB of free capacity to prevent the compiler from stopping after about ten hours with an error message.

Also, the Linux in the virtual machine must be brought up to date - in order to be able to download OpenELEC in this case; you need, for example, the git package - specifically, the following packages and their dependencies were initially

46

installed:

apt-get install git gawk build-essential gperf cvs texinfo libncurses-dev

xsltproc libxml-perl

apt-get install openssh-server

If you do not already have it, it makes sense to install an SSH server if you want to monitor the Unix machine remotely via the console. To be able to analyze and compile the downloaded sources, first, switch to the OpenELEC.tv directory.

cd OpenELEC.tv/

Then start in the subdirectory OpenELEC.tv with the command

PROJECT = RPi ARCH = arm make -j 8

Building the personal OpenELEC XBMC distribution.

In our example, after a relatively short time, an error message appeared - git criticized further missing packages on the Linux machine:

apt-get install gawk zip unzip xutils default-jre

Alternatively, in the absence of Java, the OpenJDK can be used instead of the default jre if you are developing on the Linux system.

apt-get install openjdk-6-jre

Anyway - start the compilation process by

PROJECT = RPi ARCH = arm make -j 8

again. After starting the compilation process, you can turn off the computer's screen - it will now spend several hours compiling the numerous packages, reloading other packages, and putting it together as a complete package.

Of course, it takes a bit longer to compile in a virtual machine than it did on a native machine: a VMware machine running Ubuntu 12.04, configured 1GB of memory, 20GB of hard disk capacity, and one CPU allocation Building the OpenELEC package in full configuration over twelve hours.

Also, the space required for the creation of the package is immense: Before starting, the hard drive was filled with about 3.3 GB - after compiling it was 8.4 GB more. For this reason, you should build the Linux machine and also pay attention to a sufficient hard disk equipment. Otherwise the compilation process in the dumbest case terminates shortly before the end due to lack of storage space.

After compilation, the result is stored in the directory OpenELEC.tv - here is a complete Linux distribution for the Raspberry Pi.

Prepare SD Card For OpenELEC

Like the customized Debian and Raspian for the Raspberry Pi, the memory card image for OpenELEC with two partitions must also be created on the SD memory card. However, here, OpenELEC separates like the FRITZ! Box - namely the operating system from the data area of the user -, while with the other derivatives only the / boot directory is pushed into the FAT32 partition.

Basically, the OpenELEC system with two partitions is split up as follows:

1. The first partition contains the FAT32 formatted / flash area of 128MB, usually labeled SYS or SYSTEM. In it are beside the files necessary for the boot process like

Bootlader and the like also the over 80 MByte SYSTEM file as well as the kernel.img file.

2. In the second partition formatted as ETX4, the user data is underlain. It contains the / storage area, in which not only the user data, but also XBMC Mediacenter settings, SSH settings, and much more will be saved. This partition is flexible, meaning that it does not matter whether you use a 4 GB, 8 GB, or 16 GB SD card - the storage space is also available in the / storage area.

If the SD card is plugged into the Linux computer or assigned to the virtual Linux machine, check with the command, for example

sudo blkid

or

udo dmesg

which device file the card is mounted on. In this example, it is / dev / sdb. So correct the address for subsequent commands, and possibly adapt it to your configuration. First check whether there are already partitions on the SD card.

Then unmount the SD card from the system - this is done by umount command:

sudo umount / dev / sdb

In the first step, the mentioned 128 MB FAT32 system partition is created for OpenELEC and in the second step it is marked as bootable.

Then, the second (data) partition is created, taking up all the space that is there on the SD card.

After a moment the changes are written. Now again check the (new) partitioning on the memory card with the parted command.

sudo parted -s / dev / sdb print all

If the partitions are created correctly, the next step is to format the partitions. The first, smaller partition is known to be formatted FAT32 (VFAT) while the data partition is populated using the Linux EXT4 format.

The system label is technically irrelevant - some call it sys or system, or storage or data in the partition of the data area.

To see the successful formatting of the two freshly created partitions now on the Linux system, re-initialize the partition table.

sudo partprobe

Now both partitions should be mounted in the Linux

system. In the next step you transfer the compiled data to the SD card.

Transfer OpenELEC To The SD Card

The first step is to change to the command line in the OpenELEC.tv directory, which is usually also in the directory in which you have compiled OpenELEC.

cd ~ / OpenELEC.tv

Now check whether both partitions are properly integrated in Linux

- depending on the used Linux you have to help, many of them are already done automatically.

If you already want to use a pre-compiled OpenELEC, use the bootloader files.

The use of the arm128_start.elf file for the use of the 256 MByte memory ensures that both receive 128 MByte. Since only the start.elf file is interpreted at startup, in this case save the original file with a descriptive name and rename the arm128_start.elf to start.elf.

In the next step, a file called cmdline.txt will be added to the system partition, which will house parameters for the OpenELEC kernel.

The specification of disk = / dev / mmcblk0p2 indicates the data block, the specification of the ssh parameter ensures that the built-in SSH server is also switched on immediately after start-up in order to ensure remote access. The quiet parameter hides the startup messages after turning on the Raspberry Pi. For the first attempts, you can also supplement the debugging parameter if inexplicable errors occur during startup or operation.

OpenELEC-RPi.arm-devel - *. Kernel-

The boot logo is hidden by the nosplash parameter. After writing the cmdline.txt you now transfer the actual OpenELEC files - the kernel and the system.

When copying the system files, you should pay attention to the upper and lower case: The OpenELEC-RPi.arm-devel - *. System file ends up in the system directory of the SD card with the name SYSTEM, while the file is lowercase than kernel.img is copied there.

Finally, check again if all files have arrived on the SD card. The ls -latr / media / system command should look like this:

$ ls-latr / media / system
a total of 94078
-rwx   ------ 1 root   root 2347220   2012-11-23   22:40
start.elf
-rwx   ------ 1 root   root 17764   2012-11-23 22:41
bootcode.bin
-rwx   ------ 1 root   root 88608768   2012-11-23   22:48
SYSTEM
-rwx   ------ 1 root   root 5337008   2012-11-23   22:48
kernel.img
-rwx   ------ 1 root   root 50   2012-11-23   22:49
cmdline.txt
drwx   ------   2   root   root 16384   2012-11-23 22:49
..

You can unmount the two mounted partitions from the Linux system so that you can remove the memory card.

Now the time has come to plug the SD card into the card slot of the Raspberry Pi and put it into operation via HDMI on the living room TV. Note that the first boot process will naturally take a little longer, as for example

For the first time, things like the automatic setup of the swap file, the validation of the file systems or the generation of SSH keys must be done. The creation of the data structure for XBMC is also done on the first start of OpenELEC on the Raspberry Pi.

Larger Memory Card?

The memory card capacity fdisk solution only works with the described Raspian / Debian solution. In OpenELEC and other systems, this approach fails because the partition being modified is in use and can not be edited on-the-fly. For this reason, a Unix / Linux system or a matching virtual machine with a Unix / Linux system is necessary here so that you can extend the operating system image on the SD card to the actual capacity of the SD card if there are differences after transferring the system files.

In order to be able to use the inserted SD card with the Linux partitioning tool, it must first be unmounted from the system after being inserted, ie be unmounted. Only then is she available for full access. If GParted does not exist yet, install it by apt-get. With the command

sudo apt-get install gparted

sudo gparted

start the tool with root privileges. The use of GParted is self-explanatory: If the memory card is still in the card slot, it is still readable and writable by Linux, even if it is no longer mounted via file system in the Konqueror browser.

Select the memory card from the GParted drop-down menu on the top right - a good differentiator to the existing hard disk is, of course, the capacity of the SD card. Once the card has been read, an overview of the partitioning of the inserted SD card appears.

Now you only need to mark the "last" partition in front of the free space - marked with "not assigned" - with the mouse and in the context menu of the right mouse button select the item Change size / Move.

Setting Up The XBMC Media Center

After adjusting the memory size, click the Resize / Move button. In this case, GParted creates a corresponding work order, which must first be triggered. This is like processing a batch file - then start the directory operation from the menu bar with Edit / Execute All Operations.

If you would like to make the changes at a later time or not at all, select the item Delete all operations instead. Enlarging the partition is done in a few minutes. If the Linux system does not independently integrate the SD card or the two partitions into the operating system, the command sudo partprobe is sufficient in the terminal to mount the new partitions again under Linux. Now the enlarged partition should have been allocated the complete storage space. After unplugging it again and removing it from the Linux system, the SD card can finally be used in the Raspberry Pi with the full capacity.

The XBMC interface is, so to speak, the visible heart of OpenELEC. After switching on, the system boots directly into this interface - login with user ID and password is not necessary here. If your keyboard and mouse are connected to the Raspberry Pi, you can navigate with it for now. Wireless keypads are much more comfortable - there is a wide choice here, from the small Rii radio Bluetooth keyboards to the full-fledged 105-key keyboards, which can also be operated on a notebook, for example.

ssh_enable

In our case, we had an old, cordless Logitech diNovo edge keyboard lying around in the computer corner and even found the right little Bluetooth adapter. Plugin, try it - lo and behold: The keyboard is supported immediately by OpenELEC, another additional installation is not necessary here.

After connecting the keyboard, check the SSH access to the Raspberry Pi - unlike the »normal« Raspberry Pi image, another user and password must be used with OpenELEC / XBMC. Here you use the administrative user root for the remote access, as an initial password openelec is preset.

If you have not activated SSH access using the kernel parameter, the SSH connection is switched off in OpenELEC. But it can be retrofitted through the XBMC or through creating an empty file named in the directory /storage/.config can be conveniently switched on.

Once you have successfully completed the first connection, you can either continue to work with SSH or WinSCP, or you can set up a comfortable solution via Samba that can be easily accessed from your Windows computer via Explorer or via Mac OS via the Finder to the corresponding shared directories access the Raspberry Pi or OpenELEC and edit them.

For example, to turn on Samba support for accessing the OpenELEC system, you must first enable the Samba daemon on the Raspberry Pi. This is done when the OpenELEC is started via the XBMC interface.

Customize OpenELEC settings And Set Up Shares

While formerly netmount.conf needed to include network shares, XBMC now has built-in support for NFS (Linux), Samba (Windows), and AFP (Apple) access, which makes it easy to use the makes different media and storage locations in the home network much more comfortable. Selected operating system settings and their XBMC-related services can be conveniently changed via the Programs menu of the included OpenELEC OS Settings add-on. Start the corresponding option on the XBMC with a mouse click or [Enter] key of the keyboard.

Once the add-on OpenELEC OS Settings has been started, four tabs are displayed, which you can go through step by step and whose options you can adapt to your personal requirements. In the System tab, you first set the layout for the connected keyboard. If you have a QWERTY keyboard with umlauts, choose de for the layout (German) - for the alternative keyboard layout, for example, or one of your choice. Automatic updates are disabled in this example, with the use of an LCD screen can still make driver adjustments.

The Network tab contains the current network settings. Here are the parameters of the built-in, wired eth0 network interface. If you are using a WLAN USB plug-in module, this must be configured via the Network 2 tab.

In the Hostname field, enter the name of the Raspberry Pi as it should be called in the IP network or locally. However, this has nothing to do with the Samba server name that you may know from the Windows network. You do not need to change anything in the Network Adapter field unless you have a good reason to do so. Basically, OpenELEC is configured so that it can automatically be supplied with an IP address via DHCP.

Sometimes it may be useful to assign a static IP address to the Raspberry Pi. In the next step, you switch on the access functions to the OpenELEC Mediacenter. Before accessing the Raspberry Pi system via Samba or SSH, it must first be turned on and then configured.

In the Services tab, simply switch on the Start Samba at boot option with a mouse click or keyboard. A later Samba network connection from your computer uses exactly that authentication method, so make a note of the parameters.

Administration Via The Command Line: Enable SSH Access

If the cmdline-txt-gadget does not yet create the SD card image, the SSH access can also be switched on later via the XBMC interface. And last but not least, switch on SSH access with the OpenELEC add-on mentioned above - almost mandatory for administrative purposes in the home network.

Setting Up Samba: Convenient Access To The Mediacenter

Basically, make the changes to the Samba configuration in the /storage/.config/ directory. If this file is free of errors, the corresponding original will be overwritten and used in the / etc / directory. So you have in the file storage/.config/samba.conf

If a personal, working configuration is stored for the previously activated Samba server, the default configuration of /etc/samba/samba.conf will be discarded when the Samba service is started, and the new file will be used.

The first access to the file is a bit tricky at first: After connecting via SSH, simply copy the sample file as a conf file in the console and open the created file with the well-known vi editor.

If you can handle the vi-editor, the workgroup, the NetBIOS name (netbios name), under which the shares in the Windows network are to be visible, as well as other parameters, such as additional shares, will be suitable. But also note here: Less is more - the main thing, it works first time a free-gift, but for right.

If you do not want to make any changes, or do not save them, use them to cancel the processing.

Access To NFS / Samba Shares In The Home Network

In order to be able to integrate remote shares from other computers on the Raspberry Pi or on the XBMC as if they were directly on the Raspberry Pi, you need a so-called mountpoint on the Raspberry. In principle, this is nothing more than a directory that provides the content of the network share virtually locally - namely, as long as they share in the home network can also be reached.

To do this, create in the writeable / storage area the directory or directories that should also be used in the XBMC. If SSH is enabled, connect to XBMC-Raspberry Pi and use the above commands, as in this example, two include Samba shares for video playback and an NFS share for additional music in the

Raspberry Pi.

To access other Linux computers and NAS storage on a home network from the Raspberry Pi, this access must first be turned on and configured. While better NAS systems with RAID5 have a built-in graphical configuration menu in which the most popular types of sharing such as Samba, AFP (Apple File Protocol), FTP and NFS can be set up with just a click of a mouse, this is a self-built NAS or a Linux system a little less expensive. Here you enter the directory that you want to share in the network via NFS into a so-called export file.

This can be found in the / etc. directory - open it with an editor and enter the directory that should be released for the Raspberry Pi (or for other computers in the home network). As usual with Unix systems, a certain spelling of the share is necessary in this configuration file - here you are best guided by the self-explanatory sample entries.

The / var / nfs / music directory is only released for the IP address 192.168.123.47, behind which in this example, the Raspberry Pi is hidden. After saving the file, first activate the changes with the command

exportfs -a

Then leave with the command

exportfs

Show the active NFS shares of the computer.

The console command is sufficient on the Raspberry Pi with OpenELEC. Subsequently, the content of this directory is visible in the XBMC share / storage / music2 for the Mediacenter.

Better NAS systems for the SOHO area also bring the Windows release technology in the form of Samba - the access from a Unix system using CIFS (Common Internet File System) is possible.

In the following, it is assumed that a Samba and / or Windows share already exists in the home network. This is not a big science, even under Windows. Here you select the corresponding folder, right-click Properties in the context menu, click on the tab Sharing, and then on the button Advanced Sharing. Then enter a descriptive release name and click on the OK button.

The CIFS network protocol is based on NetBIOS over TCP / IP and SMB and is part of the Samba package. The integration of the Samba shares is done indirectly on the command line with the option -t cifs. Unhide the shares as usual on the command line using umount.

All commands can be entered after switching on the Raspberry Pi on the command line via SSH. But that gets pretty annoying when it has to be done manually every time you reboot. Therefore, for the Raspberry Pi insert and XBMC, a script is recommended, which is executed automatically after every start. This autostart.sh script is stored in the /storage/.config/ directory, it is structured like a simple shell script.

In this case, the network drive will only be mounted if it is not already mounted. The output of the mount command uses grep to search for the local approval name. If this is not found there, it is first checked by ping, if the remote computer is even reachable. If so, the mount directory is created via mkdir -p (if not available), and finally the mount command is triggered. In the example

mount -t cifs //192.168.123.123/USBDisk1/storage/videos3 -o username = xbmc, password = raspi

the user xbmc with the password raspi is needed. On the other hand, if you have not set any user-level security on the Windows PC (access each one), the following command is sufficient:

```
mount                          -t                          cifs
//192.168.123.125/!_musicvideos_YT/storage/videos3
```

If the script can not be executed after autostart.sh has been created, it should first be executed once via the chmod + x autostart.sh command.

```
vi autostart.sh
chmod + x autostart.sh
./autostart.sh
```

If the newly included directories are also exported to the home network via Samba by the Raspberry Pi, the last line ensures that the "new," personal samba.conf is reinitialized.

To access the XBMC web server, OpenELEC also offers web access, which allows remote control of the system. Thus, any device that has a simple web browser can also act as a remote control on the sofa if you do not have a keyboard nearby.

```
vi ~ / .xbmc / userdata / guisettings.xml
/ Web
```

In order to activate the XBMC web server via SSH on the command line, it is necessary to intervene in the guisettings.xml file. Open it with an editor and search for the string Webserver - in the vi-editor / webserver in command-mode.

If that's too complicated for you, you can, of course also make this adaptation on the television via XBMC. Navigate via SYSTEM / Settings / Services / Settings to the web server menu:

The basic Samba configuration is also stored under XBMC. Here you should at least customize the workgroup label so that the default releases of XBMC can then be deployed on your home network.

After changing the settings, they should also become active. Here, XBMC usually requests a system reboot. By selecting Yes, this will be done immediately.

After restarting the Raspberry Pi, you can check on a computer whether the web server is running and whether logging in to the XBMC user interface is also possible.

An alternative browser like Firefox does not show this behavior and presents the web frontend of XBMC after entering username and password.

Note that you should only let the web server run if you really use it. Due to the limited resources of the Raspberry Pi, it makes sense to operate only the most necessary services for better performance.

Weather Forecast With The Weather Plug-In

If you want to be informed about the weather and the forecast for the next few days with every system, you can also activate the weather plug-in on the Raspberry Pi.

Seriously: The Raspberry Pi is more than busy with the XBMC, here we have also disabled the RSS treadmill in addition to the weather plug-in, so as not to permanently run the built-in CPU at 100% CPU utilization.

OpenELEC: Reduce High CPU Utilization

If you follow the discussions on the Internet in the OpenELEC forums on the most frequently encountered problems and demands, the topic of CPU utilization and memory utilization is on the top of the list. Here are the standard answers are always the same: disable unnecessary services, disable features such as weather frontend and RSS notifications - but the CPU load seems to remain high unabated.

Help is, however, a tip from an XBMC developer to draw attention in the right direction - as on a web page (http://thepcspy.com/read/how-fix-idle-100-cpu-issue-xbmc/) described on this topic. The reactivation of the so-called Dirty Regions should help to noticeably reduce the CPU load. If activated, only the changed menu areas will be recalculated, instead of rebuilding the entire menu on the screen.

If you are using the Samba configuration described in this book, you can easily access the network share /storage/.config via Windows Explorer, Mac OS X Finder, or other file managers. There you create a file named advancedsettings.xml. You can also do this via SSH in the console:

nano /storage/.config/advancedsettings.xml

Of course, you do not have to type the file completely. Download the file as a template from the OpenELEC project page and customize the entries.

Now restart XBMC and check if the created xml file is processed and used. In our case, we found only a slight decline in CPU utilization to 88% - not quite the resounding success. Incidentally, this was due to the fact that the resolution remained unchanged at 1,920 x 1,080. This should also remain so, since in the home network over the Raspberry Pi frequently HD streams must be transmitted and brought to the screen.

Spiegel Online, N24, Bild.de, YouTube, Süddeutsche.de and many more that present themselves on the internet and publish video material there, can also be integrated via XBMC as a video add-on. This will not only provide you with a clear overview of the videos of the corresponding offers, but also an advertisement-free and therefore comfortable presentation and navigation. The video add-ons can be easily installed via the XBMC homepage via video / video add-ons.

After download and installation, the plug-in provides the selected website as a video source.

If, for example, you have activated Spiegel Online's extensive video archive as a video source, you can first look at the sections defined there and then dig deeper into the archive from there.

In this example, the category Sport was selected by Spiegel Online, most of which was created in cooperation with the football magazine Kicker. There you will be informed daily about the events of the German Bundesliga and their clubs.

If different drives from other computers are mounted on the Raspberry Pi and also included as a share, the OpenELEC standard installation also provides the multimedia data such as pictures, videos and music in the home network for UPnP-compatible devices.

Playback of the media files over the network usually works smoothly - but when playing MPEG encoded material on the TV when playing back via the Raspberry, the screen remains black: Unfortunately, there is no indication - but in the Raspberry- Environment is well known that the Raspberry Pi simply lack the necessary licenses for MPEG playback. The subsequent purchase of the licenses makes the reproduction possible.

Submit MPEG-2 And MPEG-1 Codec

Only for the use of XBMC and omxplayer is the somewhat annoying option for playing video files that come in MPEG-2 or MPEG-1 format, here in each case the appropriate license for the decoder commercially available. These are obviously license costs that have to be paid to the MPEG organization.

To buy the right licenses, open the website www.raspberrypi.com. com / license keys /. Ordering requires the serial number of your Raspberry Pi - the code you received after the order expired. However, it is bound to the Raspberry Pi and must be specified for use in the configuration file of Raspberry Pi. To find out the serial number of Raspberry Pi, you need to open the command line via SSH and give the command cat / proc / cpuinfo

on.

After a few hours or even several days, you will receive an e-mail containing your personal code for decoding the video files while playing. To make this code known to the Raspberry Pi or the XBMC, it is necessary that you edit the configuration file config.txt and enter the corresponding code in it.

You can either get the SD card out of the Raspberry and open the configuration file via the computer's SD card slot, or you can edit the file via SSH directly during operation. With a normal Raspberry Pi you open via SSH.

In the OpenELEC system, the file is stored in the read-only / flash area. Here you first open the / flash memory for write actions and then change the config.txt file. After saving the changes, reset the write protection for the flash memory.

Just add a new line for each codec and enter it like the example code below:

decode_MPG2 = 0x56781234,0x00001234

decode_WVC1 = 0x12345678,0x00005678

Sometimes Handy: Take Screenshots

For documentation purposes and the like, taking a screenshot of the XBMC is a welcome tool that you can easily make with your keyboard attached using [Ctrl] + [S]. If no keyboard is connected to the Raspberry Pi, but only a Spartan remote control in use, you need a command line connection via SSH.

Basically, the following command is required to take a screenshot on the OpenELEC system:

xbmc-send --host = 127.0.0.1 -a "TakeScreenshot"

Alternatively, the putty / plist tool can also be used to start a convenient batch file from the Windows desktop with a mouse click. The prepared screenshots will land in the / storage / screenshots directory on the Raspberry Pi.

Chapter 6 - Raspberry Pi Practice: Projects And Solutions

Anyone who owns more than one computer these days - be it because a new one has been acquired, be it because a second one is used at home or used by the children - will not be able to tackle the issue of networking at the latest by purchasing the Raspberry Pi , The Raspberry Pi shows its strengths, especially in network operation: Regardless of where you are and whether the data you want to access it on different computers and hard disks - the Raspberry Pi provides access.

With VPN: Secure Access To The Home Network

Anyone who wants to access the Raspberry Pi and thus his or her data in the home network without spies and credentials while away from home can also use the VPN functions of the home DSL / WLAN router. Especially a product like the FRITZ! Box from AVM basically offers this possibility, but still has to be set up and configured.

After that, nothing is in the way of secure access to the Raspberry Pi. You can upload or download data, configure and use things on the Raspberry Pi, and much more. In addition, not only the data access, but also the data transfer on a release basis is possible and extremely practical - for example, when the storage capacity of the digital camera on vacation is running low, and the data can be stored easily and, above all, safe on the local hard drive.

For this purpose, apart from the correspondingly configured DSL / WLAN router with VPN functionality, only one VPN client for Windows or Mac OS X is required, which is partially available free of charge. Based on the widespread FRITZ! Box, this practical application is described here - depending on the DSL / WLAN router model with VPN functions, it can also be transferred to other models.

Setting Up The VPN Connection To The FRITZ! Box Home Network

In order to access the home network via VPN while on the move, a VPN-capable DSL / WLAN router and a special software VPN client on the notebook, Mac, or PC are required. No matter which VPN method or protocol - PPTP, L2TP, IPsec, SSL etc. - is used, both communication partners must use the same so that a connection is made. In most SOHO solutions the IPSec protocol is implemented, the corresponding key protocol ISAKMP / IKE provides the actual encryption of the connection.

In this post, the configuration of a VPN connection from a remote PC and Mac to a VPN-capable FRITZ! Box is explained by AVM. These DSL / WLAN boxes are distributed not only by AVM itself, but also by Internetproviders like GMX, 1 & 1 etc. Although the instructions refer to the original FRITZ! Box, they can also be applied to the OEM models. Basically, the following steps are necessary:

• Creating the configuration file
• Create the user-based access configuration file
• Import of the configuration file into the FRITZ! Box
• If necessary, install a VPN client and configure the VPN client using the FRITZ! Box configuration file

With the coupling of two nets the last step is omitted; here simply, the configuration file is loaded on both sides.

Create VPN Config File For FRITZ! Box

The FRITZ! Box receives its VPN configuration via a so-called config file in which the most important parameters for the connection are stored. In order to exclude typing and syntax errors here, AVM provides a wizard called FRITZ! Box Remote Access Setup for creating the config files, which can be found on the AVM web server.

However, setting up the FRITZ! Box, remote access program, is only designed for Windows operation - if no Windows PC is available in your home network, an installed Windows XP or 7/8 on the Mac is via Boot Camp or Parallels or VMware Merger mandatory ,. Alternatively, the office PC can be used - only the setup wizard of AVM must be equipped with the appropriate parameters, the installation of the configuration files is done after work at home easily via the Mac.

After download and installation, start the program FRITZ! Box remote access. Before you get started, however, you should provide the following information for the VPN configuration - missing a trifle, the VPN connection will fail.

If you are on the Internet with a dial-up connection or a changing public IP address, you need a dynamic DNS address from a FreeDNS provider. Profiusers with a fixed IP address can use the IP address instead. Now an assistant opens - there select the option Configure remote access for a user and click on the Next button.

In the following dialog, enter the e-mail address of the user in the input field E-mail address of the user. This is the username, which does not necessarily have to be an e-mail address - you can also use any username. The wizard generates the password for this user name automatically.

In the next dialog, enter the dynamic DNS domain name configured in the FRITZ! Box in the Name field. Alternatively, an IP address can be entered - Power users with a fixed public IP address at home do not need to go through the dynamic DNS name.

If the FRITZ! Box in the home network uses the default configuration for the IP address range, use the option Factory setting of the FRITZ! Box for the IP network. In this case, the FRITZ! Box provides the address range 192.168.178.0 for the devices in the home network.

On the other hand, if you have configured the IP address range according to your personal wishes, select the Use other IP network option and enter the IP network and subnet mask here.

In addition, enter here the IP address that should be given to the notebook, Mac, or PC during VPN connection setup. It is important to ensure that the IP address is not already used by any device in your home network, so it can not be confused.

Now the assistant can create the configuration files for the FRITZ! Box and the user access. This takes a little while - in the next dialog, you can choose what to do with the created configuration files next.

In order to better understand the settings, the relevant sections of the two created sample files are printed below. In the user-specific configuration file vpnuser.cfg, the dynamic DNS name (here: name.homedns.org) is entered in the target area under name / remotehostname. In addition, the user names (user_fqdn) as well as the encrypted password (key) for establishing the important connection, you always need this information, even if an alternative VPN client is used for access.

The access list specifies the IP network that is allowed to be accessed via VPN. In this case, the remote network has the range 192.168.123.0/24. If necessary, this list can be extended with a comma separated - but this is usually not necessary. If you want to restrict access to a single file server, you can do so here as well - instead of the network you can also enter a single host address.

Remote_virtualip specifies the IP address assigned to the client after the VPN security parameters have been processed. Anyone wishing to subsequently change the IP address will adapt this entry and import the configuration file fritzbox.cfg into the FRITZ! Box again to notify the change.

Import VPN Configuration Into FRITZ! Box

The FRITZ! Box allows up to five simultaneous VPN connections - each one may require its own configuration file. To import the generated configuration file fritzbox.cfg into the FRITZ! Box, first open the user interface of the FRITZ! Box via the web browser. There you can change to Settings /Internet /Remote Access /VPN. The Browse button first selects the corresponding fritzbox.cfg configuration file.

The configuration files for the VPN connection are in Windows 8, Windows 7 and Vista in the directory

% USERPROFILE% \ AppData \ Roaming \ AVM \ FRITZ! VPN \

in Windows XP in the directory

% USERPROFILE% \ Application Data \ AVM \ FRITZ! VPN \

There is a directory with the same name as your dynamic DNS domain name. In it, you will find the configuration file fritzbox.cfg for the FRITZ! Box.

In the next step, access must be set up by the remote user. For Windows users, AVM provides a special client for this, which is installed as described in the next section and set up using the configuration file.

Secure Access To The Home Network With Mac OS X

All you need in addition to the appropriately configured DSL / WLAN router with VPN functionality is a VPN client for Mac OS X, which is available for free. Based on the widespread FRITZ! Box 7170, this practical application case is described here. Depending on the DSL / WLAN router model with VPN functions, it can also be transferred to other models.

If the FRITZ! Box is equipped with the appropriate configuration file; you can also access the home network with a remote Mac. All you need is a VPN client like IPSecuritas (www.lobotomo.com/products/IPSecuritas/index.html). Unli ke other commercial solutions, IPSecuritas is freeware and is available for free download.

Start the configuration via Finder / Programs / IPSecuritas and then select connections in the menu bar. Then the following dialog appears:

In the tab General, you enter the dynamic DNS name under Firewall address under which your home network can be reached on the Internet. If you have got a fixed IP address from your internet provider instead, use it. Then enter the IP address you want the Mac to use as a local IP address on the home network in host mode.

In this example, the IP address 192.168.123.201 has been set up. This is located in the same address range as the remote home network, which in this case has been configured under Remote Endpoint /Network with the address range 192.168.123.0 and the network mask / 24 - which corresponds to 255.255.255.0. Then change to the Phase 1 tab.

Otherwise, set the Diffie-Hellman entry in the DH group to 1024 (2), the encryption to AES 256, and the authentication to the hash algorithm SHA-1. For IKE phase 1 mode, set Exchange Mode to Aggressive, see the figure for the other settings.

For local identification, set the option field to USER_FQDN and enter the user ID (here: e-mail address) in the next field. For Remote ID, set Address. Before copying the password from fritzbox.cfg to Preshared Key via copy-and-paste, make sure that the authentication method is set to Preshared Key.

After completing the configuration, close the connection window.

VPN Connection Setup And Data Exchange

The created connection is in the status window of

IPSecuritas. If you have now established an internet connection externally, simply start the VPN connection to your home network at home by clicking on the Start button.

After a short moment, the connection is established in the home network. Now the home network shares are available in the Finder.

On the other side - in the home network - the configuration page of the FRITZ! Box also indicates an active incoming VPN connection. In the overview dialog, the green light lights up for remote access.

With an active VPN connection, you can access the available file shares on the home network, such as the NAS server, the Time Capsule network disk, and, of course, the Raspberry Pi. Go here in the Finder menu Go to the dialog Connect to Server. There, you enter the protocol used and the IP address of the share.

For example, with the entry smb: //192.168.123.20, access the Windows-dows / Samba shares of the device with the IP address 192.168.123.20. If you want to open the web interface of the Raspberry Pi, use the address of your home network in the web browser - in this case, the private address 192.168.123.47.

Simple and comfortable: you sit on the sofa and discover something interesting on the Internet, which you would like to print out. So far you have sent the corresponding link by e-mail, so on the iPad or iPhone an e-mail account is configured, this e-mail on the computer opened and then sent from there to the printer. In contrast, you can use the Raspberry Pi in the future directly from iOS to send the print job to the printer - without the annoying detour via the computer. Of course, this only works for iOS applications that support print functionality, such as Mail, Photo, Safari, and more.

Raspberry Pi As An AirPrint Server In The Home Network

To make the Raspberry Pi available as an AirPrint server in the home network for iPhone, iPod touch, or iPad, some dislocations and adjustments are necessary - even when it comes to new iDevices with iOS 6 and the Raspberry Pi in operation. Since this AirPrint function was originally the purchase reason for the Raspberry Pi, this project is still talking about the Debian / Raspian version 6 - Squeezy - which is still available as a download, but now from Debian / Raspian Version 7 - Wheezy - was replaced.

Undocumented: Retrofit AirPrint

If you just want to print something quickly from the iPad or iPhone, the first push comes up against limitations: While a computer simply installs the appropriate driver, this option is not provided for an iOS device such as iPad or iPhone in terms of architecture. Even with the USB cable, you will not get far when connecting to a printer - if you have a wireless network at home, you better use wireless printing over Wi-Fi.

Since 2011, with the update of iOS 4.2.1 for iPhone and iPad, the local printer can be used directly from the hand-flatterer with the AirPrint function in the local network. However, in contrast to the original release version, the printing function has been re-cut from version iOS 5 and the new iPad and works according to the will of Apple initially only on special AirPrint printers from Canon, HP, and others.

To use AirPrint on the official way, there is no need for further installation on iPad or printer. Here you simply use the forwarding function on the iPhone or iPad and select by tap on Print the printer menu. In the next step, the device scans the home Wi-Fi network for AirPrint-compatible printers and lists them in the printer selection. Then send the print job from the iPhone or iPad via WLAN directly to the found printer.

AirPrint Printers by Apple's Grace

The special feature of a so-called AirPrint printer is that it has already integrated the necessary network print server services - here you do not need an intermediary computer, which translates, so to speak, the printout for the printer in printer language. However, with a trick, it is possible to operate a computer-connected printer as an AirPrint printer on the network - then the client computer takes care of the preparation and control of the printer.

An annoying prerequisite for this, however, is that the computer must be switched on permanently - this is depending on the computer used in terms of electricity costs an expensive fun and only in cases really recommended if the computer is already turned on. However, for the provision of a 24/7 service, the Raspberry Pi is the much better choice - and cheaper anyway.

If you do not have a printer with AirPrint function at home, you should - if it goes to Apple - make room in the study and buy a compatible printer. But anyone who already owns a printer (without the AirPrint feature) should look for a more recent firmware version from their printer manufacturer. For example, HP is constantly expanding its AirPrint-compatible printer palette, and some older printers are getting the AirPrint feature later with a firmware update. If a new firmware version is available, install it according to the manufacturer's instructions.

But in times of paperless office, many print on the home computer nothing more or only rarely enough that the printing function on the iPad will probably be used even less frequently. Therefore, the new creation of a printer just because of the AirPrint function makes no sense - here you use the Raspberry Pi and equip it with the Linux printing system CUPS, so as to provide AirPrint functions for free.

Retrofitting AirPrint Printer With Raspberry Pi

Note that once the installation is complete, a 2 GB memory

card is almost full - installing printer drivers, PDF features, and the like takes up some space. If the memory card is already getting tight, you should switch to a 4 GB memory card or larger at the latest. First, bring the Raspberry Pi up to date.

If there are too many packages to be updated, the update mechanism sometimes gets out of step and does not find the requested packages right away.

If errors occur, it helps in practice to then trigger the command via console again as a precaution. In the next step, update the installed distribution on the Raspberry Pi with the following command:

sudo apt-get upgrade

In this example, 59 packages had to be updated. Fortunately, the update mechanism tells you how much space is needed.

If there is a lot of space on the SD memory card, you should pay attention to which packages require how much space. Although Debian shares the amount of disk space the packages need to install, it does not mention that there is still room for general work and for the swap file. Side effect: Especially when you have to cope with capacity problems, this also affects the performance - the Raspberry Pi slows down.

The advantage of a freshly updated system is that you avoid any mistakes in advance. Checking for possible dependencies keeps packages reasonably up-to-date, even if they are not explicitly selected for updating.

Of course, not install update and apt-get install upgrade. If you want to operate the Raspberry Pi exclusively as an AirPrint printer and, for example, as a Samba server in the home network, you do not need things such as the graphical desktop and associated tools. Remove them - this creates space on the SD card.

Download And Install CUPS And AirPrint Features

Whether AirPrint function or not - for the use of a printer under Linux, the Common Unix Printing System (CUPS) has prevailed. Here, the printing process is divided into a print client, which sorts and forwards the print jobs, and the print server, which handles the actual printing. These include the classic

CUPS packages such as cups cups-pdf cups-driver-gutenprint also include those for coupling the hardware to provide the classic drivers.

With the large number of available and supported printers, a corresponding number of drivers are installed on the Raspberry Pi. For the AirPrint functionality later programs and services come into play, which in turn access the CUPS functions and thus control the printer. But more on that later, install CUPS from the command line with the following commands:

sudo bash

apt-get install foomatic-db foomatic-db-engine foomatic-filters

apt-get install cups cups-pdf cups-driver-goodprint

gutenprint has nothing to do with a former Defense Minister of the Federal Republic of Germany, but is a driver collection of printer manufacturers such as Canon, Epson, Lexmark, Sony, Olympus and PCL printers, which can be used after installation with Ghostscript, CUPS, Foomatic and GIMP.

If the memory card is too tight, it may make sense to check first whether the printer used is supported by gutenprint or not. In the latter case you could do without sprint print if you can get a suitable CUPS driver for your printer from the manufacturer for Debian 6.

If the storage space does not play a major role, the installation makes sense, not least for reasons of compatibility. Even if you later want to retrofit a printer, the printer may be ready for use immediately.

Owners of a Hewlett-Packard printer must install the hplip package:

sudo apt-get install hplip

sudo apt-get install pycups python2 python-cups

Then, if not already installed, install the Python scripting language and the pycups or python-cups connector, which is responsible for using the CUPS 1.2 API in Python programs, allowing Python-based programs to print.

Now the Linux printing system CUPS with printer should be installed. Now download and configure the Avahi driver or daemon, which provides the actual AirPrint functionality. If you have already installed the hplip package in the case of an HP printer, avahi and mDNS are usually already on board. In spite of this, you play it safe again and reinstall the package in case of doubt.

Mandatory: Install Avahi and mDNS server

For the actual AirPrint function you need besides CUPS still further packages, which are to be installed only after the successful CUPS installation. With the following command you get the basic packages, which in turn check their dependencies and, if necessary, reload further packages until the actual program is installed properly.

sudo apt-get install avahi avahi-daemon avahi-discover libnss-mdns

Only with the installation of avahi and libnss-mdns you make sure that the CUPS Raspberry can also perform its Bonjour function for the iOS devices in the home network. In addition to mDNS (Multicast DNS) Bonjour uses DNS Service Discovery (DNS-SD). After installation, the mDNS responder is automatically set up on the Raspberry, which answers the query and reply requests of the iOS devices.

With Tildesoft's Discovery Browser (available for free from the iTunes Store), you can use your iPhone or iPad to test the Bonjour capabilities of the Raspberry Pi installation - scanning the entire home network for Bonjour-enabled devices, so to speak.

In principle, when using CUPS, you also need an administrative user who can not only install the printer, but can also later make various settings for maintenance purposes via the CUPS configuration page. Basically, this user must also have a user account on the appropriate machine - in this case, the Raspberry Pi -; just use the existing user pi - in this example with the default password raspberry. This user must be added to the appropriate CUPS group - the lpadmin group - using the usermod command from the command line.

sudo usermod -ag lpadmin pi

If you have already set up a different username for this purpose, use it for this purpose. In the example below, we create a user named printer and password printerpassword.

sudo adduser printer

sudo usermod -ag lpadmin printer

If the user is created and a member of the lpadmin group, start CUPS for the first time in the default configuration. The installation and configuration of the actual printer or the adjustment for AirPrint will be done in the next step. First of all, it's about fixing the CUPS printing system as the basis for the next steps.

To do this, start CUPS and then start the Avahi daemon via the command line:

sudo /etc/init.d/cups start

sudo /etc/init.d/avahi-daemon start

If errors occur at the start of the two services, you must re-install the packages as described above - both are essential for the next steps.

If the CUPS daemon is running, you can log in to the CUPS

configuration page for the first time - but before doing so, you must first set the appropriate port and enable access for local clients to CUPS.

All At Home? - Configure Access To CUPS

The first port of call for CUPS configuration on the command line is the cupsd.conf file located in the / etc / cups directory. Here is an overview of the most important changes for the AirPrint access - you will find out in detail later which interventions are necessary.

Server Alias *

Port 631

Lists /var/run/cups/cups.sock

To implement the required changes for CUPS, open the CUPS configuration file with the command

sudo nano /etc/cups/cupsd.conf

Depending on the editor used (here: nano), first navigate downwards with the arrow keys until you reach the entry localhost: 631. Here, CUPS listens for jobs on the local machine (localhost) at port 631.

That's a good idea, but we want to use the printer from the entire home network, so CUPS should listen not only to localhost but basically to port 631.

For this reason, the entry localhost: 631 is commented out by a preceding picket symbol (#), and in the following line the entry port 631 is set. These changes were made with Change1-Airprint and Change2-Airprint documented.

So that the CUPS printer is visible for each device in the home network and no longer deals too sensitively with inquiries, which do not bring a correct HTTP header, the basic access for all (*) is allowed - thus also for Apple's Bonjour services or devices who use this technique.

To do this, enter the parameter ServerAlias * in cupsd.conf, if possible at the beginning. This change is documented in the figure with Change3-Airprint, the remaining three (Change4-Airprint, Change5-Airprint, Change6-Airprint) concern the access to the corresponding configuration pages on the CUPS web frontend, the admin page and the configuration files. The parameter Allow @LOCAL was set here for access. For example, if you want to restrict access to the configuration pages, it is best to use the @SYSTEM switch, which ensures that only members of the lpadmin system group can access them.

<Location / admin / conf>
AuthType Basic
Require user @SYSTEM
Order allow, deny
</ Location>

If you now want to allow access to the system from the network, this is done as in our example by Allow @LOCAL - which ensures that all computers (and the iPhones, iPads, etc.) in the local network access the corresponding CUPS service allowed. The @LOCAL parameter is nothing more than the IP address range in which the CUPS server is operated. Once the desired changes have been made, save the file by pressing [Ctrl] + [X] together with the overwrite confirmation.

sudo /etc/init.d/cups restart

Then restart the CUPS service on the Raspberry Pi to enable the changes you have made and then log in to the CUPS administration page.

Use Admin Website: Pair Printer With CUPS

CUPS has a built-in web server, accessible via port 631, which is used to set up and manage the printers. Naturally, the CUPS admin page can be reached at the same IP address as the Raspberry Pi. Anyone who does not operate a DNS server in the home network or has simply forgotten this IP address will get it on the console of the Raspberry Pi via ifconfig command. In this example, the Raspberry Pi can be reached via 192.168.123.28 - port 631 has been set in the configuration file. In effect, this means that by entering 192.168.123.28:631 in the address bar of the web browser from any computer on your home network, you will reach the CUPS summary page on the Raspberry Pi.

Now navigate to the Administration tab and release the printer to be added. Basically, it is the case with the admin page that every user is allowed to perform all actions here - if you would like to add a printer, a password prompt appears when changing. For this, you previously specified an appropriate username during setup, which is also a member of the Linux group lpadmin on the Raspberry Pi. In this example, there was the Raspberry Pi user pi and the newly created user named printer, which was also added to the lpadmin group.

Check the box when releasing printers connected to this system and click the Change settings button to apply. Afterwards, the website expects a renewed confirmation of the change. Do not be intimidated by the possibly appearing page. The security certificate of the website is untrustworthy - at the IP address you can see that this is your print server. Therefore, click the Next / Continue button on this page.

Now that you have authenticated yourself to CUPS, you can set up the CUPS printer (s) available on your home network configuration page.

Adding And Setting Up Printers In The Home Network To CUPS

Ingenious - if you have a printer with a USB interface, you can now plug it into the Raspberry Pi and switch it on. Thanks to the Raspberry Pi, you have a cost-effective print server in the home network, which you can now use from all computers at home. In addition to the printers that can be connected to the Raspberry Pi, CUPS naturally also supports printers that are located on other computers in the home network (and released there), as well as the classic network printers that come with a built-in print server and also an IP address in the home network are reachable.

No matter which printer or printer type you use - local printers connected directly to the Raspberry Pi, network-accessible printers, and printers on remote print servers are set up using the same steps in CUPS. It is only important that the printer (s) are turned on and can be reached directly or indirectly via the home network.

Start by searching the home network for available printers.

Clicking the List Available Printers button already has many devices found automatically.

Now click on the Next button and select the driver of the found printer, which should normally already be included in the CUPS package. After a few moments, a whole range of available drivers will appear.

Many drivers are often listed for a model - which of them provides the best print quality and performance is perhaps an experience you need to classify yourself. Now the printer is added to the CUPS configuration, but does it print as well? You can start the test print in the tab Printer with the respective printer via the pop-up field Maintenance with the option Print Test Page.

If a test page emerges from the connected printer in just a few minutes, you have successfully set up CUPS.

For example, to put the configured CUPS printer of the Raspberry Pi in the home network for the computers in operation, there the installation of a network printer is necessary. For example, in Windows, select Printers from the Control Panel and click the Add Printer option in the menu area to start the Add Printer Wizard.

In addition to a normal, local printer, the Add a network, wireless or Bluetooth printer option is also available. Click on the Windows network shares of the connected PCs to see the shares or shared printers.

Alternatively, you can also click on the option The printer you are looking for is not listed and select the shared printer manually by browsing. Choose these now. In the dialog that opens, enter the address of the Raspberry Pi / CUPS server in the Select shared printer name box:

http: // <IP address-Raspberry>: 631 / printers / <printer name-with-CUPS configuration>

In this example we use

http://192.168.123.28:631/printers/HP_LaserJet_2100_Seri es

After clicking Next, Windows is now looking for available drivers - and the Raspberry Pi: Here, the installation mechanism connects and offers the appropriate drivers to choose from. In this case, first select the manufacturer and then in the right window under Printer the appropriate printer model.

Subsequently, if desired, the name of the printer name can be adapted.

If CUPS has activated the corresponding drivers for the network printer, click on Next. In the next step, the printer installation assistant with a summary dialog in which you can initiate the printing of a test page.

The next step is to pair CUPS with the AirPrint peer - the Avahi Daemon - that keeps the network up to date on iOS devices.

Automatic AirPrint Installation With Python Script

In order for the changes made to remain even after a restart of the Raspberry Pi, you still need support. For this purpose, it is necessary to include a suitable script (https://github.com/tjfontaine/airprint-generate), which automatically performs this task. Here's the easiest way to bend the Raspberry Pi so that this script works the way it should - unless you're proficient in the Python scripting language. First create the necessary directory / opt / airprint and change to the directory via cd command.

sudo mkdir / opt / airprint

cd / opt / airprint

sudo wget -O airprint-generate.py - no-check-certificate https://raw.github.com/tjfontaine/airprint-generate/master/airprint-generate.py

sudo chmod 755 airprint-generate.py

Then load the script per wget directly from the author of the Python script (Timothy Fontaine) to the Raspberry Pi. Note that the above sudo wget command spans two lines. After a moment, you downloaded the 10K script.

Then set the access permissions of the Python script with the command

sudo chmod 755 airprint-generate.py

This allows the owner of the file to write, read and execute, while the group and all others are allowed to read and execute. That is completely sufficient.

Password Protection When Printing

If a user and a password are required for printing under CUPS, these must also be specified in the Python script. To do this, open the file in an editor and search for the string # air = username, password, which you comment out and then populate with the user and the corresponding password.

In our case everyone in the household is allowed to use the CUPS printer, no CUPS access protection has been activated. The next step is to generate the necessary service file for AirPrint using the downloaded Python script. The goal is here

/ Etc / avahi / services.

sudo ./airprint-generate.py -d / etc / avahi / services

Now the Python script recreates the services file and writes it to the / etc / avahi / services directory, which is completed after a moment.

iOS 6 In Action? - Retrofit AirPrint To Raspberry Pi

The previously introduced solution works smoothly for iOS 5 devices. However, since the release of iOS 6 in the fall of 2012, many of the printers have stopped appearing after the iOS 6 update, or access to the printer has run out of space. After the release of iOS 6, it was not long before the complaints in the Apple forums under apple.com up under the blanket, because Apple has again cut the AirPrint support as at the time when switching from iOS 4 to i OS 5. Here's where customization of two configuration files helps to get the CUPS printing system back on track for AirPrint.

Never change a running system: As a precaution, you should make a backup of the files to be processed, so that you can easily restore the original state if necessary.

ls / etc / avahi / services

First check the services file for the created AirPrint printer and, if necessary, save the original with the cp command. After opening the file, this shows the following contents:

<? xml version = "1.0"?> <! DOCTYPE service-group SYSTEM 'avahi-

service.dtd '> <service-group> <name replace-wildcards = "yes"> AirPrint

HP_LaserJet_2100_Series @

% H </ name> <service> <type> _ipp._tcp </ type> <subtype> _universal._sub._ipp._tcp </

subtype> <port> 631 </ port> <txt record> txtvers = 1 </ txt

record> <txt

record> Q total = 1 </ txt record> <txt record> Transparent = T </ txt record> <txt

record> URF = none </ txt record> <txt

record> rp = printers / HP_LaserJet_2100_Series </ txt record> <txt record> note = HP

LaserJet 2100 Series </ txt-record> <txt-record> product = (GPL Ghostscript) </ txt

record> <txt record> printer-state = 3 </ txt record> <txt record> PRINTER

type = 0x80901c </ txt record> <txt record> pdl = application / octet

stream, application / pdf, application / postscript, image / gif, image / jpeg, image / png,

Image / tiff, text / html, text / plain, application / openofficeps, application / vnd.cu

ps banner, application / vnd.cups-pdf, application / vnd.cups-postscript </ txt

record> </ service> </ service group>

Here the expression image / urf is missing at the end of the line:

pdl = application / octet

stream, application / pdf, application / postscript, image / gif, image / jpeg, image / png,

Image / tiff, text / html, text / plain, application / openofficeps, application / vnd.cu

ps banner, application / vnd.cups-pdf, application / vnd.cups-postscript, image / urf

However, this control is not mandatory and certainly not necessary, as this file is automatically rebuilt when the airprint-generate.py script is restarted. After all, according to the facts available, a change to two files is necessary. First, back up this by cp command:

sudo cp /usr/share/cups/mime/mime.types /usr/share/cups/mime/mime.types.org sudo cp /usr/share/cups/mime/mime.convs/usr/share/ cups / mime /mime.convs.org

Then open the mime.types configuration file, which will make the CUPS printer appear as a device on the iOS device.

sudo nano /usr/share/cups/mime/mime.types

There you add the line

image / original (0, UNIRAST)

into the file - pay attention to the distances that you create with the [Tab] key.

The same applies to the file mime.convs.

sudo nano /usr/share/cups/mime/mime.convs

There you add the line

image / urf application / vnd.cups-postscript 66 pdftops

also clean with intervals by [Tab] key in the configuration file. Once the changes have been saved, change to the directory / opt / airprint /:

cd / opt / airprint /

sudo ./airprint-generate.py -d / etc / avahi / services

and restart the AirPrint Python script. This rewrites the services file and saves it for the printer in the / etc / avahi / services directory, which is completed after a short while. Then start with the command

sudo /etc/init.d/avahi-daemon restart

Re-activate the Bonjour service on the Raspberry Pi to enable the changes made.

AirPrint HP_LaserJet_2100_Series @ raspi-airprint._ipp._tcp.local. IPP (Internet Printing Protocol)

Raspi-airprint.local: 631

192.168.123.28:631

note = HP LaserJet 2100 series

pdl = application / octet

stream, application / pdf, application / postscript, image / gif, image / jpeg, image / png,
Image / tiff, text / html, text / plain, application / openofficeps, application / vnd.cu
ps banner, application / vnd.cups-pdf, application / vnd.cups-postscript, image / urf
printer-state = 3
printer-type = 0x80901c
product = (GPL Ghostscript)
qtotal = 1
rp = printers / HP_LaserJet_2100_Series
Transparent = T
txt = 1
URF = none
If you use the Tildesoft Discoverer on your iPad or iPhone, you will receive an output when parsing the IPP (Internet Printing Protocol), in which you will now also find the required image / urf parameter.
When using AirPrint, certain functions, such as duplex printing, selecting a different paper tray, etc. may not be available.
In the menu Print ...
Select a printer ...
print options
choose ...
The print job has been issued.
After a short moment, the connected printer will go off. Now, thanks to the Raspberry Pi, you are fully equipped in your home network - in addition to the computers, thanks to the retrofitted Bonjour function, you now also print with the iDevices from Cupertino.
With Apple's AirPlay technology, content from the iOS, such as iPhone or iPad, can simply be streamed wirelessly to the

connected speakers via Raspberry Pi. The only thing you need is a wireless LAN network, speakers, and a Raspberry Pi that you can set up as an AirPlay device in minutes. Of course, you can also use the installed on the Raspberry Pi solution from a computer in the home network on which iTunes is located - but come iTunes and the iPhone or iPad from the same home.

Jack As Standard Output Device For Audio

Normally, the audio output of the Raspberry Pi is active by default. If you want to be on the safe side, the 3.5 mm jack output is fixed as a standard audio output device. To do this, use the command on the command line:

amixer cset numid = 3 1

In this case, the value 1 is in the command for the 3.5 mm headphone jack output - basically you can assign this value as follows:

Outputs value

Automatic 0

3.5mm headphone jack output 1

Audio over HDMI 2

If an error occurs (amixer: command not found), this is because in this case the audio support is not (yet) installed or has been uninstalled.

sudo bash

apt-get install alsa-utils

modprobe snd_bcm2835

Anyway - for AirPlay you need of course the audio output of the Raspberry Pi, so that the connected speakers can also be filled with music.

Then insert the driver into the system via modprobe and activate it. Then restart the configuration of the default output device for audio playback:

amixer cset numid = 3 1

In the next step, the Raspberry Pi preparations are done, now you can install the free Shairport package and put into operation.

Installing Shairport Package

First, bring the Raspberry Pi up to date and then install various packages necessary for the successful completion of the installation. Although git and perl are usually found on the Raspberry Pi - here you can get the installation for safety's sake:

sudo apt-get update

sudo apt-get install git libao-dev libssl-dev libcrypt-openssl-rsa-perl libio-socket-inet6-perl libwww-perl avahi-utils pkg-config

When you're ready to install Shairport, clone github.com's Shairport repository to the pi user's local / home directory on the Raspberry Pi.

sudo git clone https://github.com/albertz/shairport.git shairport cd ~ / shairport

sudo make && make install

sudo apt-get install pkg-config

sudo make && make install

If errors occur again, perform the installation with full root privileges.

Execute the make and then the make install command for the installation.

To do this, open a root console with sudo bash, clean up again and start the

Compile again:

sudo bash

make clean

make && make install

This process takes another few minutes.

Before you configure Shairport to your environment and start it automatically after booting the Raspberry Pi, install a Session Description Protocol (SDP) bug fix file that will allow iOS 6 devices to run successfully Shairport is necessary:

wget   http://www.inf.udec.cl/~diegocaro/talleracm/libnet-sdp-perl_0.07-1_all.deb

sudo dpkg -i libnet-sdp-perl_0.07-1_all.deb

After installing the libnet-sdp-perl_0.07-1_all.deb file via dpkg -i, the installed shairport has now been updated to the latest iPad and iPod support. Now configure Shairport for the automatic start, if the Raspberry Pi is restarted.

Setting Up Shairport

In the created source directory of Shairport is a sample file, which you also need as a startup file with a small adjustment for the Raspberry Pi. These are copied to the start directory /etc/init.d/ of the Raspberry Pi, where all startup scripts are located, and set the appropriate permissions of the file, so that it can also be executed at system startup.

sudo bash

cd /etc/init.d

cp ~ / shairport / shairport.init.sample /etc/init.d/shairport

chmod a + x shairport

update-rc.d shairport defaults

insserv shairport

In the next step, change the daemon start arguments to a name that the iPhone or iPad should later use to find the Raspberry Pi.

sudo nano shairport

To do this, customize the startup file /etc/init.d/shairport and change the entry DAEMON_ARGS there. This is originally:

DAEMON_ARGS = "- w $ PIDFILE"

Here you comment out the old entry by picket symbol and add the new one

Line on:

DAEMON_ARGS = "- w $ PIDFILE -a rAirPort"

Alternatively, you can of course directly change the corresponding line of code in the script, which is up to you.

After saving the file and quitting the editor, for safety's sake restart the shairport service on the Raspberry Pi.

sudo /etc/init.d/shairport restart

In the next step, you can connect the speakers to the Raspberry Pi and pick up the iPad or iPhone from which you want to stream music to the Raspberry Pi.

Using Shairport On The iPhone

Start as usual the music app on the iPhone and navigate to your favorite music playlist. Start any song on the iPhone - now the song should be heard through the built-in speakers of the iPhone. To redirect the audio output to the speakers connected to the Raspberry Pi, select the AirPlay icon.

If the Raspberry Pi is not visible as a speaker, start the iPhone on the iPhone Settings dialog and check if you are also in the same network as the Raspberry Pi - if necessary, deactivating and activating the network settings. Simply switch to flight mode and exit again - then the Raspberry Pi will be available as an AirPlay device.

Uses: Webcam and Raspberry Pi

If you have a zero-fifteen webcam - like a Playstation 3 - lying around, you can use the Raspberry Pi to bring it back to life and use it as a webcam, for example. Since this combination not only works, but is also economically recommendable in times of high electricity prices due to the low power consumption of the Raspberry Pi, the presented solution is all the more attractive.

Here you first install the known under Linux FFMpeg package, which is responsible for the compression of the captured images and makes them available for other applications, such as for web page transmission in a media player-capable format as MJPEG stream or simple for a remote media player like VLC on another computer.

Obtain And Compile FFMpeg

The widespread FFMpeg package is unfortunately not included in the standard package sources of the Raspberry Pi and must be added manually. Then you need to download and compile the package for the Raspberry Pi. But one by one - first add the reference source for FFMpeg to the Raspberry Pi configuration.

Edit Sources

In order to edit the package sources on the Debian-Wheezy-Raspberry, you need to have administrative privileges, which you get from the leading sudo:

sudo nano /etc/apt/sources.list

Here you add the two lines

deb-src http://www.deb-multimedia.org sid main

deb http://www.deb-multimedia.org wheezy main non-free

just add to the already existing ones.

To initialize the new sources and put them into operation, you now have one

Update with the following command through:

sudo apt-get update

Initialize sources and adjust again

Then install the deb-multimedia package from the "new" source.

keyring:

sudo apt-get install deb-multimedia-keyring nano /etc/apt/sources.list

Once done, edit the package source configuration file again and comment the line deb http://www.deb-multimedia.org wheezy main non-free using the leading picket fence icon or delete the line completely from the File /etc/apt/sources.list.

The next step is to load the sources from the actual FFMpeg

package.

Get And Compile FFMpeg Source Files

Tailor-made compiling is boring and time-consuming for the perfect adaptation to the target system, but it has the advantage that the finished solution usually works as well. First, get the sources via apt-get command:

sudo apt-get source ffmpeg-dmo

Switch to the source directory with the cd command. It's best to use the autocomplete function of the [Tab] key - this helps a lot to get you to the right destination directory.

cd ffmpeg-dmo-0.11

./configure

make && make install

With the start of the script ./configure you trigger the compilation and configuration of the existing source files, in order to then install them on the Raspberry via make or make install.

Then the FFMpeg package is ready for use on the Raspberry Pi.

Stream Audio

If you also want to transfer audio data - ie sounds - via the connected webcam during streaming, this must of course support the webcam, ie have a built-in microphone. In addition, the ALSA sound package must be installed on the Raspberry Pi.

Sound Desired? - Switch on ALSA

To do this, open the configuration file for the package sources with the nano-editor:

sudo nano /etc/apt/sources.list

and add two package sources:

deb-src http://www.deb-multimedia.org sid main

deb http://www.deb-multimedia.org wheezy main non-free

After initializing the package sources with

apt-get update

Now install the sound support after:

apt-get install deb-multimedia-keyring libasound2-dev

Then a reworking of the repositories is required - as is known, the line must

deb http://www.deb-multimedia.org wheezy main non-free

in the package file

/etc/apt/sources.list

be deleted or commented out. If not available, download the Sources of FFMpeg again on the Raspberry Pi:

apt-get source ffmpeg-dmo

go to the directory and lead with

./configure

such as make && make install

Compile and create the FFMpegs package again - this time with sound support. In the next step, you can configure FFMpeg and put it into operation.

The operation of a service or program usually requires parameters that are created in a configuration file belonging to the package. In this case, you create such a file in the / etc directory using the touch command itself:

sudo touch / etc / ffmpegserver.conf

To fill the created file with content, open it with the nano-Editor:

sudo nano /etc/ffmpegserver.conf

and add the following lines there:

Port 80

BindAddress 0.0.0.0

MaxClients 5

MaxBandwidth 50000

nodaemon

<Feed picam.ffm>

file /tmp/picam.ffm

FileMaxSize 10M
</ Feed>
<Stream picam.mjpeg>
Feed picam.ffm
Format mjpeg
Video Size 640x480
VideoFrameRate 10
VideoBitRate 2000
VideoQMin 1
VideoQMax 9
</ Stream>

The entries are self-explanatory. If you want to run the webcam on a port other than the default Web server port 80, change this value. The limitation on the number of concurrent accesses (here: 5) and the maximum bandwidth help to conserve the Raspberry Pi resources. Afterwards, a feed and the stream are created - with the latter you enter with VideoSize the values that your webcam connected to the Raspberry Pi supplies. With a meager network connection, it helps to reduce this value to 320x240. Save this file now.

So that the installed FFMpeg server also knows where its configuration lies and with which parameters or which device it should work with at all, you also create a start script that ensures that the camera runs even after a restart of the Raspberry Pi. With the command

sudo nano /usr/sbin/picam.sh

create the file - in our example we call it picam.sh - in the directory / usr / sbin and carry the configuration there

ffserver -f /etc/ffmpegserver.conf & ffmpeg -v verbose -r 5 -s 640x480 -f video4linux2 -i / dev / video0 http: //localhost/picam.ffm

After registering and saving the file, it must be made executable as usual under Linux. The easiest way to do this is with the command

chmod + x /usr/sbin/picam.sh

Now the preparations are finished, in the next step you can put the Web-cam into operation.

If the created script has execute permissions, start the script with the following command on the command line:

/usr/sbin/picam.sh

Now you can put this stream in a window in your own website or display the generated feed (here: picam.ffm) via a web browser. However, you are more flexible with a network-capable video player such as the VLC, which dominates the playback of network streams from the outset.

Raspberry Pi as Electronic Watchdog: What was a huge expense and effort a couple of years ago is now done with a Raspberry Pi and the purchase of one or two cameras directly or through the home network connected to the Raspberry Pi. Next, set up a system that lets you monitor and record 24/7 events from use as a multimedia baby monitor to house or property monitoring.

However, a permanent recording costs not only computing power, but also storage capacity - a good compromise here is to turn on the camera's motion detection on the Raspberry Pi and start the recording only when it is necessary. Or you only specify specific image areas for which monitoring is to be activated. Anyway, with the Raspberry Pi

Put together a home and property supervision, which is optimally tailored to your needs.

Install Zone Minder Via Apt-Get

For the installation of Zoneminder at least one SD memory card of 4 GB or more is recommended. Since the default image size of the Debian image files is usually adapted to 2 GB memory cards, the memory card must be adapted in accordance with the instructions, thus also providing the necessary space for the Raspberry Pi or the operating system and Zoneminder to provide.

The following sequence of commands is necessary to completely install Zone Zone and its dependent packages and to put them into operation for the first time:

sudo bash

apt-get update

apt-get install zoneminder

service zoneminder restart

service zoneminder status

After installing and starting Zoneminder, restart the Zone-less restart call to see if stopping the dependent services will work properly and restart them. You can then use the status parameter to display the status of Zoneminder on the console.

Pair Zone Children With Apache Web Server

Basically, the Apache web server is always co-installed with the Zoneminder package, even if an alternative web server is already on the Raspberry. However, apart from the system resources, Apache is a good choice for zoeminder operation, since Apache is already well configured and running at the factory. But for automated startup or operation under Apache you have to create a link to the zone minor configuration file and restart Apache to activate the change.

sudo bash

ln -s /etc/zm/apache.conf

/etc/apache2/conf.d/zoneminder.conf

/etc/init.d/apache2 force-reload

If you want to make sure that Apache or Zoneminder really works after a restart of the Raspberry Pi, start with the command

reboot

the Raspberry and then activates the root-

Access to the console:

sudo bash

In the next step you create a system user for zone-minor.

Mandatory: Create users for zone children

In order for Zoneminder to work properly after installation, it is necessary that you create a user for the application on the Raspberry Pi. With the command

sudo adduser www-data video

add the user wwww-data to the group video.

No Firefox? - Install Cambozola

As you know, not all web browsers around the world react the same, from the presentation to the format. Here, the Zoneminder developers recommend the installation of a plug-in - in this case Cambozola, which until then was known to the author only from the cheese counter. Cambozola is a Java-written plug-in that can decode multipart JPEG streams in the browser - for users of the Internet explorer thus necessary. To install Cambozola, do the following for the Raspberry Pi in the terminal:

sudo bash

cd / usr / src

wget

http://www.charliemouse.com:8080/code/cambozola/cambozola-latest.tar.gz tar -xzvf cambozola-latest.tar.gz

cp cambozola-0.92 / dist / cambozola.jar / usr / share / zoneminder

First, initialize the root environment and load the latest version of Cambozola via wget command on the Raspberry into the directory / usr / src.

/ Usr / share / zone less directory.

Now restart the zoneminder process via service zoneminder restart:

Afterwards, the zoneminder developers recommend an apt-get update and an apt-get upgrade to update the overall system as well as dependencies on Zoneminder.

Apache Fine Tuning and Bug Fix

Especially when you're on the road, you do not want to remember long domain names. Since the Raspberry with Zoneminder is more than enough busy, Zoneminder can also be used directly as the root directory for the web server, so that when entering the zone-minor front-end, the entry of the zm-abbreviation in the address is superfluous. Thus, instead of the address http: // <IP-Address / DNS-Name-RaspberryPi> / zm the call of http: // <IP-Address / DNS-Name-RaspberryPi> will suffice. For this open the file 000-default.

sudo bash

nano / etc / apache2 / sites-enabled / 000-default

There replace the entry

DocumentRoot / var / www

With

DocumentRoot / usr / share / zoneminder

such as

<Directory / var / www />

With

<Directory / usr / share / zoneminder />

and save the file.

Then restart the webserver. For this you use this command:

service apache2 restart

If the message Could not Reliably Determine the server's fully qualified domain name, using 127.0.1.1 for ServerName, appears after restarting the Raspberry Pi or the Apache daemon on the console, a small break in the configuration file httpd.conf will help:

sudo bash

nano /etc/apache2/httpd.conf

Here you add the entry at the end of the file

99

ServerName localhost

After a restart of Apache, the error message on the console should now be a thing of the past.

If Zoneminder is properly installed, the webcam models connected to the Raspberry Pi can only be used if they are naturally also supported by Debian Linux itself. If a camera is plugged into the Raspberry Pi via USB, first check with the dmesg command on the console if the camera was even recognized by the system. If so, see if the camera is also available as a so-called device link in the Raspberry Pi:

ls / dev / video *

Output:

/ dev / video0 / dev / video1

In this example, both USB ports of the Raspberry are occupied by two identical webcams (PS3 Eye camera, under 10 Euro each). If you change devices or one is not active, you will be forced to change the zoneminder configuration accordingly, as the associated / dev / video0 source is now different.

Remedy is the use of the fixed device links, which hide in / dev / v4l / by-id and / dev / v4l / by-path - here, however, there is the problem that Zoneminder does not support too long path information in the source field. Therefore, Zoneminder truncates the specified path, which by its nature can not be found.

ls / dev / v4l / by-path /

Output:

platform-bcm2708_usb-usb-0:   1.2:   1.0-video-index0
platform-bcm2708_usb-usb-0: 1.3: 1.0-video-index0

Since this device path is definitely too long for zone children, the detour helps with a symbolic link for each individual camera, which can then also be used for zone children.

sudo bash

cd /

mkdir / cam

chmod 777 / cam

cd / cam

Then create a symbolic link to the corresponding device file in this directory for the connected camera:

Here you can use a separate directory for each connected camera. With the ln command, left the directory of / cam / c1 on the long path /dev/v4l/by-path/platform-bcm2708_usb-usb-0:1.2:1.0-video-index0:

ln /dev/v4l/by-path/platform-bcm2708_usb-usb-0:1.2:1.0-video-index0 c1

Now the result of the trick can also be used in Zoneminder. Now start the web browser on the computer.

To access the web frontend of Zoneminder, simply enter the IP address of the Raspberry Pi in the address bar of the web browser. By default, Zoneminder is configured so that you can access all areas of Zoneminder without additional authentication. By default, the zone minor installation is over which IP address the Raspberry Pi uses can be found in the console via ifconfig-Command. In this example, the Raspberry Pi uses the IP address 192.168.123.47:

http://192.168.123.47/zm

If you have run the Apache hack from the section "Apache fine-tuning and bug-fixes" and use Zoneminder directly as the root directory for the web server, the zm shortcut in the address is superfluous. In this case, just use the address

http://192.168.123.47

to get to the Zoneminder overview page.

Here are some more small work to do before you get to see the video image of the webcam for the first time. First, add a new monitor (Add New Monitor button). In this new dialog box, first enter a meaningful name for the monitor in Name.

In the Source tab, first enter the created device path (in this example, the symbolic link / cam / c1) and select the Capture Method Video For Linux version 2 entry. For the camera (here: PS3 Eye) are the device format PAL and the color palette YUYV registered.

320 or 240 pixels are used for the resolution - here, the PS3 Eye camera is already at the limit. For the camera-specific values in this dialog you will find the right parameters for many models in the Zoneminder Wiki (http://www.zoneminder.com/wiki/).

If you do not already have a webcam and need a camera for the Raspberry, you will also find information about whether the model you are looking for works with Zoneminder.

If you want to connect more than one webcam to the Raspberry Pi and use it with Zoneminder, add the second webcam to the Zoneminder configuration as described above. Although technically feasible, an active USB hub can also connect multiple USB cameras (up to four) to the Raspberry, but the system performance of the Raspberry Pi and Zoneminder operation will suffer significantly. After entering and configuring the monitors, they now appear in the Zoneminder overview page - the link Montage is now also visible.

If Zoneminder is configured, the monitor does not have to be in operation, and an image can be seen on the assembly website. But even if a picture is transmitted immediately and is visible, it is advisable to initially view the log file - for reasons of the limited system resources of the Raspberry Pi.

Fix The Webcam Bug Of Zoneminder

To see the log file or the running content, simply click on the log link in the upper right area of Zoneminder to follow the system messages of Zoneminder. In this case, the recurring shared data size conflict error is immediately noticeable.

To fix this error, open the Memory.pm file that is responsible for Zoneminder's storage management with an editor of your choice - nano in this example -:

```
sudo bash
nano /usr/local/share/perl/5.12.4/ZoneMinder/Memory.pm
```

If the file is open, look for the section

```
$ arch = int (3.2 * length (~ 0));
```

and replace it with

```
$ arch = 32;
```

The most convenient option is to uncomment the entry (erroneous for the Raspberry Pi) with a picket fence symbol # and set the arch variable to the new value on the next line.

In the next step you start Zoneminder by command

```
service zoneminder restart
```

and then check the zoneminder log file.

To view the log file again, click on the log link of Zone-minder again.

Every entry in the log file - ie writing the log files with everything else - draws system resources, and these are known to be rare on the Raspberry Pi. Here you should eliminate all visible error messages, and then later think about switching off the writing of the log file in the options of Zoneminder.

Eliminate Lib-JPEG Error Message

Anyone connecting a so-called IP camera to the Raspberry in addition to a webcam connected locally to the Raspberry Pi may also come into contact with another phenomenon in the log file: Another recurring error message in the log indicates a problem in the JPEG library, but in practice - in the console - the transferred files are fine. Another reason to eliminate the error message here and to clear the log file of Zoneminder.

In the first step, you get the download link to download the JPEG sources via wget command to the Raspberry Pi. Just look for the filename jpegsrc.v8d.tar.gz on your computer, or use the browser to go to www.ijg.org/files. There is the file or even a more recent version to find - load it now via the console of the Raspberry with the following command in the home directory of the user Pi.

wget http://www.ijg.org/files/ jpegsrc.v8d.tar.gz tar -xzvf jpegsrc.v8d.tar.gz

After unzipping by tar command, navigate to the / home / pi / jpeg-8d directory and open the file jdmarker.c with the nano-Editor:

sudo bash

/ Home / pi / jpeg-8d

nano jdmarker.c

There, use the key combination [Ctrl] + [W] to search for the string if (cinfo-> marker-> discarded_bytes) and comment, as shown in the following illustration, by entering the comment characters / * and * /

WARNMS2 (cinfo, JWRN_EXTRANEOUS_DATA, cinfo-> marker-> discarded_bytes, c);

out.

After changing the source code, create your own version of the custom JPEG package. First, prepare the available sources

./configure

on, then in the next step with

make && make install

to compile the JPEG package.

In the next step, replace the original ones with the newly compiled Lib JPEG files. To gain easy access to the files, do the following: Start a root shell, exit the Zoneminder service, make a backup copy to make any changes you can undo, and copy the two files to their new location:

sudo bash

service zoneminder stop

mv ./usr/arm-linux-gnueabi/lib/libc.so.8 ./usr/arm-linux-gnueabi/lib/libc.so.8.old

```
mv    ./usr/arm-linux-gnueabi/lib/libc.so.8.4.0    ./usr/arm-
linux-gnueabi/lib/libc.so.8.4.0.old
cp         ./home/pi/jpeg-8/libc.so.8         ./usr/arm-linux-
gnueabi/lib/libc.so.8
cp        ./home/pi/jpeg-8/libc.so.8.4.0        ./usr/arm-linux-
gnueabi/lib/libc.so.8.4.0 service zoneminder start
```

After restarting Zoneminder, the JPEG errors should now be a thing of the past. If you want to upgrade the Raspberry to an apartment / home monitoring center, Zoneminder now has all the options that would go beyond the scope of this book.

Pair IP Camera with Raspberry Pi

Cameras for indoor and outdoor use can be done easily - and these are not even expensive: So can be found in the 50-Euro price range consistently usable models, which in the featured Zoneminder configuration (almost) immediately put into operation can be.

If the budget for the purchase of an IP camera is in the 50 Euro price range, you usually end up with different models of China models, which are generally identical, but from different manufacturers and dealers different platforms such as Amazon, eBay etc.

Thus, the manufacturers EasyN, Foscam and Wansview with the same camera models with almost the same scope of supply on the market - in October 2012, however, with price differences of up to 20 €. In this example, the IP camera NC541 / W of the manufacturer Wansview at Amazon for 57 euros was the winner - the technical equivalent, for example, the Foscam FI8908W camera

Commissioning the IP Camera

No matter which camera you choose in this price range, all have in common is that the initial setup according to the will of the manufacturer on Windows is done. A preconfiguration of the camera is necessary, among other things, since this is ex works in its own subnet (192.168.0.X), and the IP address is entered there permanently.

Either you temporarily change the IP address of your computer to use it in this subnet as well, or you can use a Foscam camera tool on Mac OS (www.foscam.de/index.php/foscam-service-and -support / download / viewdownload / 19-software / 15-ip-camera-tool-for-mac), with which you can adjust the IP address of the IP camera. If the camera is unpacked and set up, it basically has the following settings on delivery:

IP address: 192.168.0.178

http: port 80

Username: admin
Password: 123456

For Windows and Mac OS X, use the camera tool to customize the camera's network settings. After the download you start the tool, which then performs a search for the camera in the home network. After a short moment she is already found.

After clicking on the camera found in the home network, a configuration dialog appears in which you can either statically adjust the IP address for your home network or set the check mark in Obtain IP from DHCP server so that the camera automatically sends the dynamic IP address from the camera local DHCP server of the router relates.

Once the IP camera is in the "correct" network, changes will no longer be a problem in the future since the camera has its own administration interface. There, the default password 123456 for the admin user can be changed to a secure password.

In the next step you open the configuration page of the IP camera - simply enter the IP address in the address field of the web browser.

The most important thing is behind you now. The IP camera is now in the same
subnet like the Raspberry Pi running Zoneminder. But a look behind the scenes cannot hurt, maybe there are new opportunities here.

Basically, after signing up, it immediately becomes apparent that the camera offers two different modes depending on the web browser. Mode 1 is for computers with Internet Explorer usage, Mode 2 is for the Firefox, Chrome and Safari competitors. The third option is for mobile devices - in the following, only mode 2 (Firefox, Chrome, Safari) will be used.

First, it checks whether the IP camera is even up to date in terms of firmware and user interface. You can find out in the Maintain tab under Device Status. The language mix is probably due to switching to a different language on the home screen.

In terms of firmware and version of the web interface, it would be nice if you knew if the version used is the current - for lack of a corresponding note in the user interface or in the documents in the box but the Internet must be consulted later.

Now, the first thing to do is to put the camera into operation, however: Basically, in places where an IP camera is to be used, only a suitable RJ45 network socket is available. Thus, the establishment or functioning of the WLAN is the first obligation of a passable wireless LAN IP network camera. Switch to the Network / Wireless Lan area.

Click on the Scan button to check the surrounding area for available WLAN networks. If the suitable wireless network with the matching SSID has been found, mark it and set the corresponding encryption of the WLAN router.

The surprise follows immediately: Here already failed the connection to the wireless router - despite the latest firmware version of the FRITZ! Box router. After several attempts and changes, the cause of this ominous behavior was quickly found: The associated password, ie the key of the WLAN connection, must not contain any special characters in this case.

This is surprising since the use of special characters dramatically increases the security level of such passwords. In this case, however, it means for now: bite into the bullet or waive the wireless feature. If you still have the sour taste in your mouth, the next relevant configuration dialog could cause heartburn in some people already: The adaptation of the dynamic DNS address is anything but user-friendly and confidence-inspiring.

In this dialog, you could enter the dynamic DNS name of the

camera if it should be accessible exclusively from the Internet. As a rule, however, this task is already performed by the connected DSL / WLAN router in the home network.

Unclear is the option Do not enable as long as the host name has not been released. Does this mean that errors in DynDNS usage are to be ignored by the camera if the configured DynDNS address is not reachable? In addition, it is unclear when the actual activation of the host name or the release takes place here. Besides, the address 002ndpr.nwsvr.com stands out here. If you search the internet for the domain name nwsvr.com, you'll soon see where this domain hides:

Now everyone should decide for themselves if they want to use this DNS address to control the external access to their IP camera at home.

In this example you should at least remove the entry at Manufacture's Domain and also leave the DynDNS service of the camera switched off first. This is not necessary for zone-minor operation under Raspberry Pi. But in principle, the direct Internet access to the camera for the security-conscious is inadequate: Here, the camera offers no possibilities - neither SSL nor other encryption technologies. So the parsing and reading the data packets including appropriate passwords for the camera access is not a big science, since the unsafe HTTP protocol is used here.

Basically, access to the camera should be controlled via another computer in the home network such as the Raspberry Pi, or it should be a security solution such as a VPN tunnel o. Ä. "Built around it" to prevent public access to the IP camera.

For operation with zone minors you create a new user in this dialog. In this dialog, it is called raspi and assigned to the user group User. The password used here is raspi123456.

For the Zoneminder project now the essential steps are done - security conscious change nor the default password for the camera admin admin from 123456 to any password. In the next step, add the IP camera to the zone minor configuration and integrate it into the monitor view

Pair IP Camera with Zone Minder

The entry of the IP camera takes place when the zooninder is started via the web front end by clicking on the link Add New Monitor. In this configuration window you first enter a meaningful name for the camera in the General tab under Name. Here the simple term entrance was chosen. For the source type, Remote / Remote is the correct entry, and for Enabled / Enabled, check the box to enable the camera for zone children. In the Source / Source tab, select HTTP for communication from the IP camera to the Raspberry Pi for the transmission protocol.

Here you adapt the host name and, if necessary, the corresponding port for the transmission from the IP camera to the Raspberry Pi.

Depending on the configured port of the IP camera (here: 8088), enter it in Remote Port / Remote Host Port - for the remote host name use the syntax user: password @ <ip-address-of-ip-camera>. If you have created a user (User: raspi, password: raspi123456) to access the IP camera, as in the above example, use the syntax raspi:

raspi123456@192.168.123.44 - in this example, 192.168.123.44 is the IP Address of the IP camera in the home network.

With Remote host path / remote path enter /videostream.cgi, for the color depth you use 24-Bit and for the video format first 320 x 240 pixels.

If the devices connected in Zoneminder are configured properly, this is indicated by the color-coded status.

After clicking on the OK button, the IP camera now appears as an additional camera in the zone minor configuration. A moment later, the status of the newly configured camera in the Zoneminder frontend changes to the color of the already confi gurated devices.

Clicking on the montage link in the Zoneminder overview, all camera images of the devices connected to the Raspberry Pi should now appear.

More pixels, more picture quality: In this configuration example, however, we had the condition that the two webcams connected to the Raspberry Pi were configured with a resolution of 320 x 240 pixels - it was only by switching from 640 x 480 pixels to 320 x 240 pixels that the IP could be switched Camera to be co-persuaded to work with the other two local cameras. Obviously, Zoneminder does not support mixed mode of cameras with different image format configuration.

Zone Fine Tuning: More Bandwidth, More Quality

The more cameras are used with the Raspberry Pi and Zoneminder, the more power and bandwidth are needed for smooth playback. Here, the type of use is crucial: Video / image recordings require in this case more I / O resources and less CPU power - a motion detection, however, is comparatively very CPU-heavy and writes less for the SD card.

Using the raspi-config command, you can use the Overclocking command to start the overclocking dialog of the Raspberry Pi. For stability and analysis reasons, you should first start with smaller overclocking steps.

So if you are planning a surveillance system primarily with motion detection (for example, a door viewer), the decent overclocking of the Raspberry Pi brings a perceptible performance kick. Conversely, it pays to buy a larger and faster SD card, if it comes to bumping now and then when saving the files.

Even with longer recordings, it happens that the available space on the Raspberry Pi is not enough. Here you should make sure that the directory / var / cache / zoneminder is sufficiently dimensioned. If you have a NAS server in use on the home network, you can also redirect this zone minor directory (and others) to the network drive via a symbolic link.

Here, the reconfiguration of Zoneminder makes sense to be able to use the storage paths of the home network and the shares available there. Alternatively, you can of course also use remote FTP directories and folders - but these must first be made known on the Raspberry Pi via mount.

Electronic Watchdog On The Raspberry Pi

Whether you operate a locally connected webcam or an IP camera on the Raspberry Pi, both of them can also be configured via Zoneminder as motion detectors and, based on this, they can subsequently do other defined things - for example, notify certain persons or secure the evidence. If Motion Detection is activated in Zoneminder, Zoneminder basically activates the complete camera image.

For example, if you were monitoring your front door, it would also monitor your house ceiling, and depending on the detection sensitivity configured, every fly fall in the image will be reported as a new event - whether or not someone is at the front door. For this reason it makes sense to set a fixed image area for permanently installed cameras for monitoring, not only to avoid false alarms but also to save space for the events.

Basically, every connected camera, which should act as a motion detector, must be reconfigured accordingly. In the Zoneminder main window, select an existing monitor. The following options are available for the function:

Now, if motion detection is switched on by switching to Modect, click on the small, inconspicuous zone link on the right-hand side of the website at the corresponding device. This will take you to the configuration dialog and then define one or more motion detection zones in the image area.

On the right in the image in the Zones column, there is a link behind the number that allows you to specify one or more zones for each device connected and configured with Modect.

Enter a descriptive name for each area that you want to record using motion detection. Here you basically adopt the settings from the following dialog - the configuration Fast, high sensitivity is shot beyond the target for some applications. This even registers the movement of a housefly as a movement - enough reason for you to experiment with the settings.

After aligning the camera, you can simply use the coordinate system of the motion detection grid to specify the corners until exactly the image area to be monitored is selected.

After defining a zone, click the OK button in the configuration window above to return to the initial dialog. If desired, you can configure additional zones for motion detection by clicking on New Zone.

After defining the zone, additional areas to be monitored can be added by clicking the New Zone button.
Less is more: After setting up the zones in the image, the configuration becomes active immediately. Any movement in this area triggers an action and thus costs resources in terms of storage space, CPU and memory load, which are not endlessly available in a Raspberry Pi. For this reason you should - before you turn up quality and bandwidth here - optimize the settings.

If necessary, consider whether the camera really needs to produce a 24-bit color image or whether a grayscale image is sufficient. In this case, the memory and CPU requirements and thus the transmission bandwidth on the Raspberry Pi would be relieved noticeably. The number of cameras used on the Raspberry Pi also plays a role: More than two devices should not be configured with motion detection activated or even with the recording function in this case.

Better accessible IP cameras over the network are the so-called PTZ cameras, which bring along features such as Pan, Tilt, Zoom (pan, tilt, zoom). Here, the range of services and quality varies depending on the capital employed - but the cheaper price range does not require optical zoom. Whether with or without zoom - with Pan / Tilt support implemented, the Raspberry Pi also lets you use the remote control features of the camera with the Zoneminder installed.

Open the device settings via Zoneminder, there is still no dialog for the control functions of the camera to find.

The remote control functions must first be activated explicitly with the zone-minor options in the system register with a check mark in OPT_CONTROL. After the zoneminder restart via service zoneminder restart, Zoneminder is available for the PTZ function.
After ticking, Zoneminder points out that changes will only become active after the restart.

Zoneminder already includes a small set of preconfigured controllable PTZ cameras in the basic installation, each of which can be found as a Perl module in the directory / usr / share / perl5 / ZoneMinder / Control /. If necessary, a suitable control module is included for your camera - to find out, the Zoneminder Wiki (www.zoneminder.com/wiki/) is a good place to start.

Conclusion

Thank you for making it through to the end of *Raspberry Pi 4: Project Ideas Book*, let's hope it was informative and able to provide you with all of the tools you need to achieve your goals whatever they may be.

One of the central goals of the creation of Raspberry Pi was the educational end - to provide children with an early interest in computing and programming. Hence the Raspbian base installation includes Scratch and Python, two interesting ways to enhance programming language learning.

Raspberry Pi is not just about the operating system, so the app store - the Pi Store - was recently launched.

One of Pi Store's goals is to motivate young people to create programs and monetize them, as not all downloadable resources are free.

Among the dozens of resources available is the free office application suite, the CodeBlocks programming IDE, and Open Arena, a game based on the Quake III game engine.

What Is It Possible To Do With A Raspberry Pi?

Although initially developed for educational purposes, innovative and interesting projects have been emerging over the last few months, using this micro-computer as a starting point:

- Arcade game machine
- Musical instrument
- Computer cluster
- SmartTV
- Home automation
- Media Center

We hope this book gave you a better insight into Raspberry Pi and how you can have fun with this amazing program.

Finally, if you found this book useful in any way, a review on Amazon is always appreciated!

Description

In recent years, two platforms have gained immense popularity in the electronics world. Thanks to Raspberry Pi, everyone can start creating interesting electronic projects! This book will introduce everyone to this extremely popular single-board computer.

What Is Raspberry Pi?

Raspberry Pi is the most popular mini credit card size computer in the world! Thanks to the relatively low price and huge possibilities, it quickly gained millions of fans. On a small board, we can find among others 4-core processor, RAM, USB, Internet, and HDMI connections. The latest version (used in the course) is also equipped with a WiFi and Bluetooth module.

In addition, the board has universal GPIO terminals to which various electronic components can be connected (eg diodes, buttons, sensors). The producer has also prepared a connector through which a camera can be connected to the popular Raspberry Pi.

Raspberry Pi is a small computer with outputs that allows easy connection of electronic components, eg temperature sensor.

Who Is The Raspberry Pi Book For?

The book has been prepared for everyone. No knowledge of Raspberry Pi, programming, or Linux systems is required. Knowledge of basic electronics concepts is welcome, but not a prerequisite!

Rasberry Pi has numerous applications! To take advantage of the possibilities that a Raspberry offers us, you need to take the first step and learn the basics of working with this computer. This book begins with Raspberry Pi's complete fundamentals: from system installation (in many ways), through necessary configurations and expert use of Linux, to universal GPIO ports.

So order your copy and start learning today!!!

Made in the USA
Las Vegas, NV
02 December 2020